Praise for *Muff*

'A seriously intriguing play.' – Paul Rodda, *Barefoot Review*

'Moves deftly between gritty realism and almost surreal horror.' – *StageMilk*

'As explicit and confronting as its title.' – Patrick McDonald, *AdelaideNow*

Praise for *MinusOneSister*

'A tough and insightful look into the interaction of the public and private spheres … Ancient Greek myths have been at the centre of many works about generations of trauma in recent years in Sydney — there's a lot of focus on our inability to effectively tackle the cycles of domestic violence right now — but Barnes' play is one of the most successful examinations of the way younger people are defined by their family history.' – Ben Neutze, *Daily Review*

'Anna Barnes does a masterful job of updating Sophocles' *Electra* to discuss some of the pressing issues of our time.' – Katharine Rogers, *ArtsHub*

'[Barnes'] poetic language borrows from Greek theatrical traditions and combines it with the speech of today, for a fascinating and modern take on the dramatic form.' – Suzy Wrong, *Suzy Goes See*

Praise for *SHIT*

'Provocative and tragic, bracing and bitterly funny.' – Cameron Woodhead, *Age*

'A vital piece of theatre, superbly constructed, brilliantly executed.' – Maggie Morrison, *Observer*

'Cornelius's new play is an outright provocation, as the title suggests. It dares to put three female characters on the stage who are rarely, if ever, given a theatrical voice. Rough, rude and irrevocably damaged, they are the kind of people most theatregoers would cross the street to avoid but, under the rich talents of the playwright … they make a compelling and heartbreaking subject.' – *TimeOut*

'This is assured and accomplished writing, where the playwright's uncompromising political vision forces us to question our assumptions about theatre and society.' – *Victorian Premier's Award judges*

'The best written and made piece of local theatre in the Sydney Festival program so far, Patricia Cornelius' unblinking study of three underclass women hits you like a slap in the face.' – Jason Blake, *Sydney Morning Herald*

Muff
Van Badham

MinusOneSister
Anna Barnes

SHIT
Patricia Cornelius

Currency Press, Sydney

CURRENCY PLAYS

First published in 2017
by Currency Press Pty Ltd,
PO Box 2287, Strawberry Hills, NSW, 2012, Australia
enquiries@currency.com.au
www.currency.com.au

Copyright: *Introduction: The Obscenity of the Feminine* © Alison Croggon, 2017; *Muff* © Van Badham, 2016, 2017; *MinusOneSister* © Anna Barnes, 2016, 2017; *SHIT* © Patricia Cornelius, 2016, 2017.

Reprinted 2019.

COPYING FOR EDUCATIONAL PURPOSES

The Australian *Copyright Act 1968* (Act) allows a maximum of one chapter or 10% of this book, whichever is the greater, to be copied by any educational institution for its educational purposes provided that that educational institution (or the body that administers it) has given a remuneration notice to Copyright Agency (CA) under the Act.

For details of the CA licence for educational institutions contact CA, 11/66 Goulburn Street, Sydney, NSW, 2000; tel: within Australia 1800 066 844 toll free; outside Australia 61 2 9394 7600; fax: 61 2 9394 7601; email: info@copyright.com.au

COPYING FOR OTHER PURPOSES

Except as permitted under the Act, for example a fair dealing for the purposes of study, research, criticism or review, no part of this book may be reproduced, stored in a retrieval system, or transmitted in any form or by any means without prior written permission. All enquiries should be made to the publisher at the address above.

Any performance or public reading of *Muff*, *MinusOneSister* or *SHIT* is forbidden unless a licence has been received from the authors or the authors' agent. The purchase of this book in no way gives the purchaser the right to perform the plays in public, whether by means of a staged production or a reading. All applications for public performance should be addressed to the author c/- Currency Press.

Cataloguing-in-publication data for this title is available from the National Library of Australia website: www.nla.gov.au

Typeset by Dean Nottle for Currency Press.
Cover design by Alissa Dinallo for Currency Press.

Currency Press acknowledges the Traditional Owners of the Country on which we live and work. We pay our respects to all Aboriginal and Torres Strait Islander Elders, past and present.

Contents

Introduction: The Obscenity of the Feminine
   Alison Croggon   vii

MUFF
   Van Badham   1

MINUSONESISTER
   Anna Barnes   45

SHIT
   Patricia Cornelius   109

Publication of this title was assisted by the Commonwealth Government through the Australia Council, its arts funding and advisory body.

Brad Williams as Tom and Claire Glenn as Eve in five.point.one's 2013 production of MUFF in Adelaide. (Photo: Olivia Zanchetta)

The Obscenity of the Feminine

Alison Croggon

Woman is literally a monster: a failed and botched male who is only born female due to an excess of moisture and of coldness during the process of conception.

Aristotle

There's not a single moment when the three young women transcend their ugliness. There's no indication of a better or in fact any inner life. They don't believe in anything. They're mean, downmouthed, downtrodden, hard bit, utterly damaged women. They're neither salt of the earth nor sexy. They love no-one and no-one loves them. They believe the world is shit, that their lives are shit, that they are shit.

Program note for SHIT, by Patricia Cornelius

If only progress were actually a thing. If it were, women writing plays about women would be as unexceptional as men writing plays about men. And yet even now, half a century after the second wave of feminism, it remains true that to contemplate the female body outside the purview of the male gaze remains a radical act.

It's not an accident that over the past decade much of the most exciting new Australian theatre has come from women and queer theatre makers. From the profound queer theatre of director Adena Jacobs, to the Rabble Theatre's confronting explorations of abjection, to the formal playfulness of Lally Katz, female artists have been breaking open the aesthetic and intellectual conventions that underlie how we make and witness theatre.

One of the most striking things about this body of work is its variousness. By exposing how gender profoundly shapes our perceptions and behaviour, women and queer theatre makers are challenging every aspect of what it means to make a performance and what it means to work within a tradition. It's no surprise that each of the plays in this book—*SHIT* by Patricia Cornelius, *MinusOneSister* by Anna Barnes and *Muff* by Van Badham—is completely different from the others, with its own aesthetic and thematic concerns.

Cornelius takes as her subject the most damaged women in our society, marginalised by poverty, sexual violence and the systemic brutalisation of state care. Barnes's archetypal family is rich and privileged, like that in the classic Greek tragedy which she uses as the springboard for her own work. Badham's play is about the sexual violence lurking inside the intimate relationships of three middle-class characters.

Put together, they make a fascinating trilogy. In each of these plays, women are looking back. What they each represent in different ways is the obscenity that exists at the heart of femininity.

It's a truism that the canon of Western art has, for the past few centuries, been the art of men. Men made the art, men owned the art and men determined which artworks were significant. Women—or perhaps, more properly, Woman—has existed in art either as an idealised object, exemplified by the iconic nude or the madonna, or as the personification of monstrosity, closely related to death. The feminine, as Julie Kristeva says in her classic study *Powers of Horror*, is abject. Woman is the source of idealised desire, but the feminine is also everything that the masculine subject seeks to eject from its own definition of selfhood: weakness, ambiguity, fluidity, and maternal and sexual horror.

Almost all of our most famous fictional women—Anna Karenina, Lady Macbeth, Nora Helmer—were written by men. Behind this is the pervasive assumption that artistic brilliance is a masculine property. The 19th-century writers who survived the heavy social prohibitions against creative women were considered exceptional and transgressive. Like George Sand they were 'masculine', not proper women at all; or like Elizabeth Barrett Browning, in the terminology of the day, a celebrated invalid, they were considered too physically frail to withstand the fires of creative genius. By embracing artistic creation, they became at best oddities: women who betrayed the function of their womanhood.

It's a shame we can't relegate these attitudes to the archives of the 19th century. Two centuries later, they are flourishing. Women still struggle to reach parity with men in all areas of artistic creation, as subjects and as artists. Art by women, especially if it's art about women, is still considered a specialist sub-branch, of interest only to a specific audience. The experiences of women still struggle to be granted the universality that is habitually granted to the experiences of men.

This, of course, extends to all categories habitually labelled 'other'. White able-bodied male heterosexual cis subjectivity is still the default authority, and that is inevitably both rooted and reflected in notions of authorship in a self-confirming spiral. It's one thing to recognise the concept of the imperial male gaze in all axes of art and life, it's quite another to undo centuries of internalisation, to actively question and reconstitute what constitutes female subjectivity and agency.

One way to begin is to look squarely at the obscenity of the feminine. This obscenity exists in two ways: in the violence, overt and covert, which polices the limits of acceptable femininity; and in the concepts of femaleness and femininity themselves. The three plays in this book examine the obscenity of femininity in both these senses.

Anna Barnes's *MinusOneSister* uses Aeschylus's trilogy *The Oresteia* to examine the structures of patriarchal violence within a nuclear family. The action in *The Oresteia* is sparked by the sacrifice of Iphigenia by her father, Agamemnon, to ensure good winds for his ships in his war on Troy. This in turn provokes Clytemnestra's revenge killing of her husband, and Clytemnestra's murder, in revenge for his father, by her son Orestes. Clytemnestra is the archetypal monstrous woman: in turn a monstrous wife, a monstrous mother who must be killed by the young hero, and, in the form of the Furies, a supernatural monstrosity who hounds Orestes from beyond the grave.

In *MinusOneSister*, Barnes focuses on the siblings, creating an uneasy theatrical space in which the classical tragedy intersects jarringly with contemporary banalities. The crimes of the parents are visible only in their effects. This foregrounds Iphigenia's death, which is a swiftly forgotten footnote in the original texts. Iphigenia becomes a toxic absence, paralleling the way violence against women remains at the periphery of vision in contemporary society.

Van Badham's *Muff* examines intimate violence in a play that appears at first to be a conventionally realist drama about a love triangle. Eve returns home to her flatmate and former lover Tom after an absence in China. Tom is in a new relationship with Manpreet, a young woman who has confrontingly internalised the sexuality of porn. As the play progresses, the realist convention begins to shift and break until we're unsure what has actually happened, or even if Manpreet exists, and it becomes clear that this is a play that examines how sexual violence traumatically splinters the subjective selves of men and women.

While the first two plays concern themselves with the privileged, Patricia Cornelius's *SHIT* is about people with no privilege at all. These women are, as Cornelius makes clear, incapable of transcending their situation: they are 'utterly damaged', the unacknowledged detritus at the very bottom of society. Yet in Cornelius's unsentimental hands, her characters are capable of agency, and they are culpable. They have internalised every misogynistic aspect of the society around them, and the lateral damage they deal out is brutal, yet they remain sympathetic, funny and likeable. We're not asked to feel sorry for them: we are asked to contemplate them as subjects, just as we are subjects. And if we do, we can see that their viciousness is familiar. The forces that have damaged these women can't be outsourced to the déclassé: it's an endemic part of the structures that shape us all.

A paradox of making this kind of art is that, time and again, the normative critical gaze snuffs out the critique embedded in the work. Conscious aesthetic choices are often rendered as flaws or faults or, which is perhaps worse, aren't noticed at all. Perhaps the most famous example of this phenomenon is the premiere of Sarah Kane's first play *Blasted*, which directly connected domestic and sexual violence to the viciousness of civil war. It was greeted with a tsunami of critical outrage at its 'excessive' violence. 'Even now,' said *Guardian* critic Michael Billington, in the 2001 mea culpa in which he revised his initial negative opinion, 'I think she overstates her case.'

This could only be said by a man who hasn't thought about what domestic and sexual violence, in its brutal physical effects on human bodies, actually is. It's this erasure of psychic and physical realities that these plays seek to challenge. In contemplating these monstrous women, they are asking us to consider what is actually monstrous. Maybe it's not these women, after all, but the forces that cause them to exist.

Melbourne
February 2017

Alison Croggon is a Melbourne writer and critic. In 2009 she was named Geraldine Pascall Critic of the Year for her theatre criticism.

Muff
Van Badham

Van Badham is an award-winning writer of more than 30 internationally produced plays for stage and radio. She has had plays and musical theatre staged at six Edinburgh Festivals, in London, and on the UK touring circuit, as well as in America, Canada, Iceland, Germany, Switzerland and Austria. Australian theatre companies who have commissioned her work include MTC, Malthouse, Griffin, Merrigong, HotHouse, Terrapin and the Tasmanian Theatre Company. International theatre commissions include Wilma Theater (Philadelphia), Bern Stadttheater (Switzerland) and Luxi Ltd (UK). Van's radio commissions have been for the BBC World Service, Radio 4, and Radio 3, and her first screenplay, *We Come Home*, was developed with a grant from the Australian Writers' Guild.

Her most recent Australian theatre productions include *The Bloody Chamber* (Malthouse), *The Bull, the Moon and the Coronet of Stars* (Griffin, Merrigong and HotHouse), *Big Baby* (Terrapin), and *Late Night Story* (Adelaide Fringe). Her first film, *Octopus*, won the first Jameson Screenwriting Award in 2008. Her first novel, *Burnt Snow*, was released in Australia in September 2010.

Van is a former Literary Manager of the Finborough Theatre London (2009–11) and was Artistic Associate at the Malthouse Melbourne (2011–13) before moving to her present position at the *Guardian Australia* as a columnist and Melbourne arts critic. She has received numerous awards for her writing and was named one of Australia's ANZ / AFR 100 Women of Influence in 2016.

Muff was first produced by five.point.one at The Bakehouse Theatre, Adelaide, on 10 May 2013, with the following cast:

EVE	Claire Glenn
MANPREET	Serena Moorghen
TOM	Brad Williams

Director, Alison Howard
Designer, Myf Cadwallader
Sound Designer, Tristan Louth-Robins

The three acts (*Muff*, *Trip* and *Meal*) can be performed in any order at the director's discretion.

A slash (/) denotes an overlap. If it appears in a line of dialogue or stage directions, it indicates that the following text is simultaneous to the text after the next slash (in the line immediately following).

Muff

CHARACTERS

>EVE, 30s, an English teacher, recently returned from China, flatmates with Tom
>TOM, 30, a venue manager
>MANPREET, 26, Tom's girlfriend

SCENE

>Eve and Tom's flat in Kilburn, North London.

TIME

>*Muff* takes place five years after *Trip* and a year before *Meal*.

SCENE 1

The bathroom of the flat shared by Eve and Tom. EVE *is in the shower.* TOM *walks in.*

TOM: Babe—

    EVE *showers.*

  Babe—

EVE: [*she can't hear him*] Tom?!

    TOM *decides to knock on the glass of the shower.*

TOM: Eve—Eve, babe—

    EVE *turns off the shower.*

EVE: What do you want?
TOM: She's here.

    No movement.

  She's here. She's upstairs. If you want to meet her—

    Pause.

EVE: I'll see you up there.

    She turns the shower back on.

SCENE 2

The sitting room of Tom and Eve's flat. MANPREET *is here. While she and* TOM *talk,* EVE *dries herself—unseen, with some kind of sadness. She will dress. She will walk out to meet them.*

MANPREET: She doesn't want to meet me, mate.
TOM: Of course she does.
MANPREET: She hates me already.
TOM: No—
MANPREET: She should be out / here—
TOM: / No—
MANPREET: —out here with a floral bouquet and a packet of biscuits. This is shocking.

This shocks me. Your new flatmate hates me and she hasn't even met me, man. In the fucking shower. Who fucking showers? I don't fucking shower.

TOM: That's because you're a very, dirty girl.

MANPREET: You'd better believe it. [*Rummaging through a noisy plastic bag*] I brought biscuits. I know how to make a good impression. Argy cow.

TOM: She's just in the shower.

MANPREET: Want a Jaffa cake?

TOM: What'd you buy?

MANPREET: Jaffa cakes! Are you deaf or blind? *Do you want one?!*

TOM: Calm down.

MANPREET: I'm calm.

TOM: You don't need to—

MANPREET: Don't tell me what to do.

TOM: She's just in the shower.

MANPREET: I'm not nervous. I don't get nervous. She can fucking hate me and it doesn't mean shit. I know what I am.

TOM: Give me a Jaffa cake.

She does.

What else did you buy?

MANPREET: Skins and Ting. And a *Playboy*.

TOM: What for?

MANPREET: To skin up, to drink and to read. After we eat the Jaffa cakes. Or during.

You're thick sometimes.

TOM: *Playboy*?

MANPREET: I've read it since I was fifteen—it's a good mag! Better than *Glamour* or *Marie Claire*. You might see real tits in a *Playboy*.

TOM: Unlikely.

MANPREET: Do you read it?

TOM: No.

MANPREET: Then how would you know?

Pause. He kisses her.

TOM: Fuck, you're hot.

MANPREET: I am.

TOM: I can't wait—
MANPREET: We could go in there now and fuck. She's not gonna walk into your bedroom. ''Ello, Evie, I'm Manpreet, I'm fucking Tom. What a nice cock he's got.'
TOM: Keep your voice down.
MANPREET: You'd be the only man in the world who'd say that—
TOM: She's just—
MANPREET: —in the fucking shower. I want the awkwardness over and done with, *done with.*

> *He kisses her again.*

You have got a nice cock.
TOM: Tight jeans—
MANPREET: Nice, fat, hard cock—this causing you pain?
TOM: It will.
MANPREET: Me not even touching it and it's causing you pain?
TOM: They're tight jeans!
MANPREET: Just me telling you you've got a nice cock and you'll get an erection.
TOM: That and you sticking your tongue in my mouth.
MANPREET: What were you like when you were fourteen, mate?!
TOM: Messier.
MANPREET: You can shove it into me later. Nice—fat—hard—cock—you can shove it into me now. I ain't got no pants on, Tommy. My tits in your mouth and your *fat cock—*
TOM: She's coming up the stairs!
MANPREET: The second she leaves this room and I'm gonna fuck you so hard.
TOM: I know!
MANPREET: We are gonna fuck all afternoon!

> EVE *appears in the doorway.*

Hi there! I'm Manpreet and you're lady Eve.
EVE: Of course. I'm sorry I was in the / shower—
MANPREET: / Don't worry about it.
EVE: I was expecting you a little later / so I—
MANPREET: / I was supposed to have a meeting but I / cancelled.
EVE: / No excuse, I should have—

MANPREET: [*smiling*] Yeah, you should have—but you fucking didn't!

Awkward silence.

EVE: Jetlag has destroyed my sense of humour—

MANPREET: But you do have one—

EVE: Somewhere. I hope I didn't leave it in Tianming. I've got a suitcase with too many pockets. It's probably in the same place as my plastic compass and emergency kagools.

Be patient with me.

MANPREET: Maybe.

Slight pause.

TOM: [*to* EVE] Do you want a—

Pause.

—Jaffa cake?

EVE: What are your plans for the afternoon?

MANPREET: We're gonna skin up and fuck.

EVE: [*to* TOM] I'll leave you to it.

[*To* MANPREET] It was nice to meet you. Have a nice …

Beat.

… fuck.

MANPREET: If you insist!

Slight pause.

EVE: I'm sure we're going to be great friends.

She walks out of the room.

MANPREET: That wasn't scary.

TOM *kisses her.*

SCENE 3

Eve's bedroom in the Kilburn flat. She's drinking wine. EVE *is talking to* TOM—*he appears during the speech.*

EVE: When I arrived in China, I—there was an American in my training group. Then two Irishmen who were on teacher exchange. An Australian I met in an expat bar. I had a one-night stand with my translator when I got to Tianming and … You can get *anything* you like in

China. All of these people—it's funny—no, Tom, it *is* funny—all of them had the same hair. Fat blokes became thin blokes, tall blokes were short blokes and Chinese, Irish, American—they all smelled like piss and vomit and bathroom tiles and metal. I drank and drank and drank and drank and drank. The more people you fuck, the lonelier you become, and a mountain village in north-east China was—

TOM: A bar near Bank station.

EVE: For a while.

She laughs.

Do you want me to stop?

TOM: Yes.

EVE: It wasn't your fault.

TOM: It certainly wasn't yours.

EVE: I'm fine, though. I'm back. That was the challenge that I set myself. Look at me now, I'm here, in your flat—I'm drinking wine!

Silence.

Elsie phoned and told me there's a room in her sister's house in Baron's Court.

TOM: You don't like the room here?

EVE: We're deluding ourselves that this can work. Living together—

TOM: It's a warm, safe place where you can rest and I can—

EVE: But that's not your job anymore.

TOM: We're older. We're different. When you came here and you were just off the plane—I hardly recognised you. You're thinner, you're darker—

EVE: Darker?

TOM: Laughing at—

You can't live with a bunch of students in Baron's Court.

EVE: They're not students.

TOM: And I think it would be—

EVE: What?

TOM says nothing.

I lived on my own on a mountain in China.

TOM: If it doesn't work out—

EVE: I'll go back to China.

TOM: That's a bit extreme.

EVE: At least I can get laid there.
TOM: This is all temporary—and we'll be fine. London's fine. You just need to click back into it.
EVE: Click.
TOM: Manpreet understands that you're still adjusting.
EVE: Click! Click!
TOM: She's very—she's twenty-six but she's not in other ways.
EVE: She's very pretty, Tom.
TOM: She's gorgeous. And super-bright. Really, really bright.
EVE: I heard you shagging this afternoon. From downstairs. Screaming—
TOM: I've spoken to her about that.
EVE: It's actually unbearable.
TOM: I'm sorry.

> EVE *drinks.*

She's been with this bloke for two years, now they've finally broken up and—I knew we'd get together but it's been tense for months. I think she's worth it.
EVE: You haven't told her about us, have you?
TOM: No.
EVE: Are you going to?
TOM: No.
EVE: I'm thinner. I'm darker. It never happened. Everything's okay.

> TOM *kisses her head and leaves.*

SCENE 4

The sitting room at the Kilburn house. EVE *is here.* MANPREET *comes in, wrapped in a duvet. She's looking for something.*

MANPREET: Good morning!
EVE: Hello.
MANPREET: I hear you think I fuck too loudly! Sorry about that. I am loud, though. Lungs of a whale.
EVE: Are you looking for something?
MANPREET: Skins. Tom wants a post-coital spliff. Tell me we were quieter. Than the other day. I've been making an effort.

> *Beat.*

I know you and Tom were together.

Pause.

EVE: What did Tom tell you?
MANPREET: He didn't. But I know.
EVE: It was a long time ago and it didn't mean anything.
MANPREET: Did you like China?
EVE: Some parts more than others. You don't have to entertain me—Tom will want—
MANPREET: [*rolling a joint*] You went to uni together.
EVE: In Sheffield.
MANPREET: I slept with all my friends from university.
EVE: Where are you living now?
MANPREET: Camden.
EVE: I don't know what Tom's told you—
MANPREET: He doesn't need to rent the room. It's been empty since Ben moved out.
EVE: London hasn't been my home for a long time.
MANPREET: Why not?
EVE: Because I was raped. Has that happened to you?
MANPREET: When I was fifteen.
EVE: Have you told Tom?
MANPREET: Don't be stupid.
EVE: He stayed in contact, when I ran away.

/ TOM *enters, in a robe.*

/ You know what this city's like—you change your email address and you can—lose people.
TOM: They're under the coffee table.
MANPREET: What?
TOM: Skins. [*To* EVE] Get a good sleep last night?
EVE: A better sleep.

EVE *sees the* Playboy *on the coffee table. Shock.*

What's this?

She picks it up.

[*To* TOM] Do you read this now?
MANPREET: It's mine. What's the big deal?

EVE: You read this?
MANPREET: It's good mag! [*Noting* EVE's *expression*] Don't they have masturbation in China?
TOM: [*to* EVE] You've never been into porn, have you?
MANPREET: *Playboy*'s not porn. You won't see more than gash-flaps.
EVE: [*flipping pages*] Their breasts up to their necks. They've all got the same face—
MANPREET: So?
EVE: Not one of them has pubic hair.
MANPREET: No-one does, mate.
EVE: The men who read this want to see women with the the the of little girls?
MANPREET: You've obviously never done it cos otherwise you'd know. Yeah, the regrowth's annoying but the sex is amazing. [*To the silence*] I get waxes all the time! They are *bitchin'* for your sex life, believe—
EVE: How? Bitchin'? / How?
MANPREET: / Men just really like it. Ask him!
EVE: [*to* TOM] Would you really kick a woman out of bed for having pubic hair?

From left: Serena Moorghen as Manpreet, Brad Williams as Tom and Claire Glenn as Eve in five.point.one's 2013 production of MUFF *in Adelaide. (Photo: Olivia Zanchetta)*

MANPREET: You get more oral sex, they're right in there—I think it's because they can see more, need a machete to cut through the forest with / some people—
EVE: [*to* TOM] / *Answer—me!*
MANPREET: *He* likes that I go through it cos I do it *for him*—He shows me his appreciation—I fucking love it!
EVE: [*to* TOM] You like the plastic tits, too?
TOM: [*of the magazine*] They're attractive girls.
EVE: What kind of fuck is a man who wants a woman to look like a kid?!
MANPREET: People have their own taste, love.
EVE: Everybody reads this. Everybody watches porn, everybody believes this is what you're supposed to look like, you pay someone to pour hot wax down your gash, tear out the hair till it bleeds and because everyone does it, if someone sees a gasp of *hair* between my legs, I'm unnatural, I'm unfuckable. Because I don't look like a ten-year-old girl.
MANPREET: You've been on some fucking mountain, lady, because [*displaying the magazine*] this is not weird. You are.
EVE: You make yourself look like a child so men will like you.
MANPREET: Go back to the seventies, have all your useless principles sprout out of your muff—he thinks my bald cunt is sexy, he thinks it's hot that I like porn, he puts me on a leash and he spanks me—

> EVE *flings her attention to* TOM.

—and it's a lot more fucking empowering than waving a placard with a bunch of withered lezzos, making sourdough bread out of yeast infections and measuring my pubes to see if I'm feminist enough. I'd much rather be what I am than an uptight, frigid bitch.
EVE: [*to* TOM] Can you *speak?!*

> *He can't. He leaves the room.*

SCENE 5

The bathroom. EVE *enters the shower. Water pours over her head. She slumps against the walls of the shower. She softly beats her head against its walls. In the background,* TOM *is fucking* MANPREET. MANPREET *is loud.* MANPREET *is so loud that* EVE *can hear her, even in the shower.* EVE *beats her head against the shower walls—chanting:*

'*Stop ... Stop ... Stop ... Stop ...!*' *She chants and slams her head so hard that her forehead cracks open. Blood on the glass.* TOM *has his orgasm.* EVE *slumps in the shower.*

SCENE 6

Tom's bedroom. He is sitting on his bed, wrapped in a sheet.
EVE *enters, wearing a robe.*

TOM: You're surprised by what you like, sometimes.
    Nic Bennett and I had beers the other day. He got pretty pissed and he told me that his girlfriend's been fucking him with a strap-on for a year. He wanted to fuck her up the arse, she said she'd do it if he did—and he got a taste for it. It's not a big deal. We're older. There's weird stuff in the sex part of the brain. I'm a venue manager, not a psychologist.
EVE: You could not love that *child*.
TOM: When you came out of hospital—
EVE: You don't want to talk about this—
TOM: When you came out of hospital—Oh God. To know—to know the worst thing I could do was desire you. They told me—
EVE: I know what they told you—
TOM: That I could rip you open. That I could—tear the stitches.

    Pause.

To love you was to divorce myself from you, sexually, safe from any association with—
    I did not want to be a tall man made short, an Englishman made—whatever he was.
EVE: He was English.
TOM: Living together was a bad idea. I'm sorry. Maybe I wanted—
EVE: Can you be in love with someone you don't want to fuck?
TOM: No. I thought that's why you left the country.
EVE: You still love me.
TOM: You staggered out of that bathroom and blood was smeared all over your legs. His cum on your thighs and the scratches. Your lip was torn at the corner—blood from your forehead, in your hair. Crying without making any noise and the heel had come off your shoe. You had it in

your hand. You had it gripped in your hand all the way to the hospital and …

He takes a breath.

… I can fuck her for all the reasons I can't fuck you. Fuck her in ways I'd never let myself imagine—

She wants me to hurt her, and I do it. I hit her and tie her up and— other things she begs me to do—

EVE: What things?

TOM: Things I can't talk to you about.

EVE: Why not?

TOM: Because I like it.

Beat.

She loves what I do to her more than she'll ever love me.

He stops himself from continuing.

EVE: Come to bed with me.

TOM: I can't.

EVE: You love me.

TOM: You're not listening.

EVE: What's wrong?

TOM: No—

EVE: I'm healed. The stitches are out, I've been with loads of people—

TOM: I don't want to.

EVE: We made love in that cold, dark room in your parents' house and you said it was like a tidal wave destroying the sand.

TOM: Five years ago—

EVE: We fucked on every surface of my apartment. The Lanes', up against the wall. In that French hotel. Your fingers up my skirt on buses, on trains—what's wrong?

TOM: Eve—!

EVE: I don't look like the girls in magazines. Is that the problem?!

TOM: No.

EVE: What's wrong with me?!

TOM *doesn't answer.*

During the following, two realities are staged at once: EVE*'s and* MANPREET*'s.* EVE*'s reality happened chronologically* *before* MANPREET*'s, but they are played simultaneously.* TOM *is caught between the two realities;* MANPREET *is oblivious to* EVE*; and* EVE *is able to see but not participate in* MANPREET*'s world with* TOM.

MANPREET *enters, fastening herself into a dress we've already seen* EVE *wear. It is Eve's dress and* MANPREET *has 'borrowed' it.* MANPREET*'s hair is done like Eve's.*

I can make myself what you want me to be.
TOM: You're being childish.
MANPREET: [*in the dress, calling out to* TOM, *who's beyond a door*] I'm ready!
EVE: Tom—!
MANPREET: [*shouting*] You coming in or what?

TOM *leaves* EVE*'s reality and enters* MANPREET*'s.*

TOM: [*to* MANPREET, *of Eve's dress*] Nice.
MANPREET: Don't get any cum on it. I won't have time to do a specialist clean before she gets in from work. You ready?

TOM *hesitates. He nods. He ties her hands above her head to something. Eve's dress has been 'borrowed' for a sex game.*

TOM: Starting now?
MANPREET: Go for your life.
TOM: You lived on a mountain in China.
MANPREET: I have fucked that many blokes.
TOM: I've dreamed of fucking you. You look so hot.
MANPREET: [*pretending to be* EVE] Dreams just confuse you. Here I am. You can have everything.
TOM: [*starting to fuck her*] I love you, Evie.
    Evie, I love you so much.

Trip

CHARACTERS

EVE, late 20s
TOM, late 20s
MANPREET, early 20s

SCENE

Tom's flat in Kilburn, London.
A cellar toilet in a pub near Bank station.
The spare bedroom in Tom's mother's house, Conwy, Wales.

TIME

Trip takes place five years before *Muff* and six years before *Meal*.

PROLOGUE

EVE *enters a dark, blank space. It's a bathroom, but we don't necessarily know that. A shower cubicle is here. She's walking through a memory.*

EVE: Pub carpet, the noise—vision blurs, I am in a house that's shaking. Buffeted and shoulder touches shoulder touches—'Excuse me'—touches elbow—'If I can—' wiping the hair from my face and there's the door, there's an arrow—'Excuse me'—and a girl in front of the door with a black plastic straw against her lips. She has honey blonde hair. / She's got glossy teeth and the boy that she talks to there's the arrow there's the door. Stairs. I am in a house that's shaking and I have to grip the handrail it's a spiral and quieter and girl on the concrete staircase—her ankle twists under a black high heel I see the bone of her ankle strain against the skin—triangular point of her shoe, she grips my arm and we both sway, we both sway, we both sway—such a laugh, this—the concrete staircase and she's heavy. She grips the rail. She stands. Fluorescent light I am grey, her skin is grey. Rubs her ankle she's got brown hair in a bob and she smiles and says, 'I've had too many'. Nod. Smile. Metal handrail. She ascends. I descend. Metal handrail. Her shoes clack clack stumble on the staircase above me. The door swings. Sound of the crowd breathes out, in.

She laughs.

Another staircase. Cold walls make the stairwell cold. I'm frightened. I'm drunk. There's the door to the ladies' toilets. I'm inside. I'm frightened.

/ TOM *appears. He is listening to her, but he is not in her reality.*

Pause. EVE *looks at* TOM.

[*To* TOM] Tom, why am I frightened?

SCENE 1

Tom's sitting-room in the Kilburn flat. TOM *has keys in his hand. This is earlier than the incident that* EVE *has just related. They have just returned from a trip.*

EVE: I think your sister's really lovely. You're clearly the golden child—she's that bloody pregnant and they drove all the way from Norwich to Wales for a day and a half—and he seems really nice. I know she drives you mad sometimes but your mum—

> *They look at each other.* TOM *looks away, jangling the keys in his hand.*

I hate it when you do that.
TOM: Do what?
EVE: Pulse with the keys.
TOM: I pulse?
EVE: Stuffy in here. You think Ben went away for the weekend?

> *Pause.*

Was he going away?
TOM: I don't know.
EVE: Something's wrong—
TOM: I don't know if I'm thirsty or not.

> *Pause.*

> *He pulses with the keys.*

EVE: Put them away.
TOM: I might go out.
EVE: We only just got home.
TOM: To the SupaSave. I need—
EVE: What?

> *Pause.*

What do you need?
TOM: Something to drink. Some fresh air.
EVE: I'll open the windows.

> *She gets up to do so. He doesn't move or respond.*

Tom?
TOM: Don't—
EVE: You want fresh air. Go to the shop. If you're thirsty, I can put the kettle on, or I can drill a hole in the ground—you're not even listening—
TOM: I don't want an argument.

EVE: Give me some instructions. Please. I had a tough weekend up there, *for you* and—weird on the drive, now you don't want to talk to me, you don't want to—
TOM: I'll go to the SupaSave. I'll be back in a bit.

He doesn't move.

EVE: Do you want me to leave?

TOM *puts his hands on his eyes.*

Oh, God.

He doesn't move.

Oh, God. You're breaking up with me.
TOM: Eve—
EVE: It was a test. It was a test and I failed it.
TOM: You didn't.
EVE: She said something—
TOM: She didn't.
EVE: I knew your mother didn't like me. I don't have the *'what?'* for her? The the the manners the breeding I'm too shy the she thinks I'm a drunk I drank too much when we got there. *Oh, God—!*
TOM: Evie—
EVE: A whole weekend in nowhere and all the things I cancelled and you're breaking up with me because I'm not I'm not I'm—you said—you said—
TOM: I love you. Calm down.
EVE: You said—
TOM: I want a drink. I need a rest. [*Frustrated*] You have your own home to go to.

EVE *lets out an involuntary sob.*

Maybe you should spend some time at yours.

SCENE 2

Back in the bathroom of the flat. TOM *is here.* EVE *is here but isn't looking at him.*

TOM: Eve's brain ... It's a cinema projector that doesn't switch off and me—

Pause. EVE *is sleeping.*

Blank. Not even white space. She dreams—every night she dreams and her soft body—

EVE *gasps—her body shudders awake.*

—bolts into spasm— [*To her, as if it's just happened*] Baby?

EVE: Concrete stairs. Fluorescent light—

TOM: It's a dream.

EVE: I tripped—

TOM: Go back to sleep.

EVE: I was wearing black shoes with a pointy toe and—my ankle!

TOM: —back to sleep!

EVE: —my ankle!

She closes her eyes again. The following takes place with EVE*'s eyes closed.*

TOM: Eve has nightmares. We'd been together for about two years when I … I wanted her to meet Mum. We hired a car and drove to Conwy, where the folks live. Maybe it was sleeping in a strange room or / a strange bed but she …

EVE: / The beach was made out of rocks and shells. Outcroppings of the rock, caves under them.

TOM: You're thinking of when we went / to—

EVE: —the / water of the ocean was colourless. There was no / tide.

TOM: / I woke up because she was sweating. It's the north coast of Wales—the house was like a block of ice and / we were naked in bed and Eve's flesh was melting.

I mean it was literally melting and sweating so much it was like I was swimming on her not lying next to her and—

EVE: / A girl was on the beach. A thin girl. Black hair. There was a crowd of people—dark and ragged—everyone's old. Everything's ancient.

TOM: What's going on in there that does this to her?

EVE: [*to the invisible girl*] What's under the cliff there?

TOM: / She was mumbling and I could see she was struggling with something—her hair was matted—matted with sweat and the sheets were like film on her—these stupid blue sheets of Mum's stuck to her skin and—

EVE: [*to the invisible girl*] / Tell me what's under the cliff! [*To* TOM] She wants me to go with her! What do I do? Tom!
TOM: When she didn't sleep properly, I didn't sleep properly.
EVE: [*screaming*] Tom!
TOM: Screaming, screaming my name and I've got her by the shoulders and—I need some water.
EVE: Don't leave me!
TOM: I've got to get some water.

He fetches himself a glass of water.

EVE: I'm asleep. There's darkness in there. An end to everything. All the evil that I've done. The rock over my head. I'll be in there forever. I'm going into the cave. I'm in the army of the dead.
TOM: [*returning*] Evie, you need some water.

EVE *is frightened by his touch, falls out of her dream.*

Drink some water.

Pause. She drinks.

EVE: That was a bad one.
TOM: I never dream.
EVE: Everyone dreams. You just don't remember them.
TOM: Is it this room?
EVE: It's not—
TOM: I'd open a window but it's freezing outside—it might be snowing.
EVE: I don't want your mother to think I'm a maniac.
TOM: I'll open the window—
EVE: Did I wake her?
TOM: Wake her?
EVE: Check. Please check.
TOM: You didn't wake her.

He checks.

Drink some water.
EVE: It was the cliffs of Arbroath. Where we went.
TOM: I remember where we went.
EVE: And it was Brighton, when we used to go there, when I was twelve or thirteen. It was dark. There was a dead child.
TOM: Don't think about it.

EVE: I don't want your mother to think I'm a maniac.

He holds her. Dark swallows them.

SCENE 3

Tom's sitting room. TOM *has keys in his hand. This is earlier than the incident that* EVE *has just related. They have just returned from a trip.*

EVE: I think your sister's really lovely. You're clearly the golden child—she's that bloody pregnant and they drove all the way from Norwich to Wales for a day and a half—and he seems really nice. I know she drives you mad sometimes but your mum—

They look at each other. TOM *looks away, jangling the keys in his hand.*

I hate it when you do that.
TOM: Do what?
EVE: Pulse with the keys.
TOM: I pulse?
EVE: Stuffy in here. You think Ben went away for the weekend?

Pause.

Was he going away?
TOM: I don't know.
EVE: Something's wrong—
TOM: I don't know if I'm thirsty or not.

Pause.

He pulses with the keys.

EVE: Put them away.
TOM: I might go out.
EVE: We only just got home.
TOM: To the SupaSave. I need—
EVE: What?

Pause.

You need something to drink or some fresh air.
TOM: Yes.
EVE: No!
We've been here before.

TOM: It's my flat, darling—of course we've been here before.
EVE: We've had this conversation.
TOM: / Surely.
EVE: / *This* exact conversation. My God. I think we're breaking up. You're going to ask me to stay at mine. God.
TOM: That's not happening. / It is not happening.
EVE: / It is!
TOM: Evie, I've had a long drive. You don't drive. I am tired, I need a drink, I am not breaking up with you. I am not.
EVE: Your keys pulse in your hand. I tell you that I've failed—and—
TOM: Failed?
EVE: With your mother.
TOM: You didn't fail with my mother. She really liked you.
EVE: Not the other time.
TOM: You've only just met her for the first time—
EVE: The other time! The other time! In the—
TOM: In the what—?
EVE: The other place—the other time—when this happened before—this has fucking happened before—here—in here—you and—you want to go the SupaSave you want me to stay at mine—I've failed / with your mother and you want to break up with me—
TOM: / Whoa! Whoa! Whoa!

Pause.

Whoa! Evie, Jesus!

Long pause.

EVE: I must be tired, too. I didn't sleep well last night.
TOM: I was there.
EVE: And I was trying so hard—to be everything she could want.
TOM: You're everything that I want.
EVE: Am I?
TOM: And Mum knows this. Everyone knows this. Even you. Come on.
EVE: What's wrong with me?
TOM: It was important to me—yes, it's important to me that you got along and you did. When my father left when I was ten years old and Mum had to be both my parents. Until she met Frank I was it in her life, I am not embarrassed by that. I'm sorry if I put—I put too much pressure—

EVE: She likes me.
TOM: That's what she said.
EVE: When?
TOM: This morning, in the kitchen. She was sorry you didn't get a better night's rest.
    She wondered if it might be the cats—they get into that room and they're all over the bed—
EVE: I woke her up.
TOM: It's okay.

    TOM *stands there. Silence. He begins to pulse his keys.*

EVE: That's exactly what you were doing. In the—the before, the dream—
TOM: I must do it all the time.
EVE: You want to go to the SupaSave.
TOM: Now that you've suggested it, I do. It's bouncing around in there and it tastes like Ting and biscuits. Do you feel like some—?
EVE: Some—?
TOM: Ice-cream? Ting? Jammy Dodgers? Baby, it's déjà vu. It's all it is. You had a dream last night.
EVE: A nightmare.
TOM: Deep and disturbing, and the electrical currents in your brain are running like breakaway trains. We had a lot to drink before we went to bed, and you're overtired and it's normal. It's a normal response to emotional pressure—which I have said I am sorry for—and your brain … It's like a hard drive, defragging—you're defragging. That's what dreams and all of this other shit is—
EVE: Not my dreams—
TOM: You're not fucking psychic—you are—under pressure / *I am fucking sorry*—
EVE: / —a maniac.
TOM: —*I am sorry, the weekend was my* / *whole idea*—
EVE: / I didn't mean. / I'm sorry—
TOM: / *I want you to meet Mum—I am in love with you*, I am not breaking up with you, for Christ's sake—
EVE: I'm sorry—
TOM: Do you think I'd drive all the way to *fucking Wales* to break up with you?

EVE: Please don't get angry.
TOM: A year I was with Victoria and she never met Mum.
EVE: I know.
TOM: She never did.
EVE: Maybe we're both maniacs. Go to the SupaSave. Get some ice-cream. I'll calm down. Get chocolate chip.
TOM: I love chocolate chip.
EVE: [*rallying*] We'll drink some wine!
TOM: It's after eleven.
EVE: It's quarter-to. That South African red that we both like.
TOM: Yes.
EVE: We'll relax, drink wine and eat ice-cream and have sex.
TOM: Or we could just have sex.
EVE: Not until we're relaxed.
TOM: [*a single pulse of the keys*] Ice-cream and wine!

He searches for his wallet, which is not in his pocket.

EVE: What have you lost?
TOM: I can't find my / wallet—

Brad Williams as Tom and Claire Glenn as Eve in five.point.one's 2013 production of MUFF *in Adelaide. (Photo: Olivia Zanchetta)*

/ MANPREET *enters the living room.* EVE *screams. She screams and screams.*

What is it?
EVE: [*to* MANPREET] Go away!
TOM: Evie! Stop screaming!
EVE: [*to* MANPREET] Get the fuck out! *Get fucking out, get out!*

    TOM *starts to disappear.*

  Tom, get rid of her—get her out! Go away! Tom!

      TOM*'s gone.* MANPREET *is* EVE*'s whole reality.*

No—! [*Hysterical*] *Tom!*

SCENE 4

TOM *in the bathroom.*

In a separate bathroom, a separate reality, EVE *stands naked in a shower. As* TOM *speaks, water begins to pour in the shower, and runs over the glass, obscuring* EVE. *She puts her hands on the glass—she's trapped, but the water increases its flow, thickening against the glass until* EVE*'s body becomes indistinct, until she fades into darkness.*

TOM: I mean, I *vaguely* might have registered she was going to the bathroom.

    I was working for a catering business in the City—this is before I got the job at the Green Note—it's what—

    Scott was Australian—he'd come to London as an actor, ended up on a moped delivering sandwiches to merchant bankers but he was good at it. He got a part back home, so it's his leaving do. I really liked him, she liked him. But it was great, he's on a soap after delivering sandwiches for a year of his life and we all went out to this big pub near Bank station. Drink, drink, drink, good friends and some interesting new people and we sank pint after pint and—we hadn't eaten, cos we'd come straight from work.

    Some bloke—solicitor—was talking up his politics and he'd been hitting on to Evie all night and we were bantering—got into an argument about Blair this and it was all about Evie he was a wanker really and where is Evie? Drink—where's she gone then? Drink,

drink. Here's the round edge of the table I'm leaning on, the beer's slightly warm because I've had more than a few and I'm drinking this one slowly—'Blah blah Blair, let me tell you'—she must be in the bathroom or something. Drink. She's a big girl. She'll be alright.

They have two sets of women's toilets in this bar. One upstairs and one right in the bowels of the building. I don't know if she even knew there were ones upstairs—she can hold her drink, Evie, but—

They reckon he would have been watching her when she was still upstairs with me. Foam of a warm beer, the edge of a glass. The woman I love is descending a staircase with a random behind her, a random with his mind made up what he's going to do this evening and she 'Blair, politics' she 'My wife' she 'at Chambers' she—

Turned the door handle the sink's in front of her—she wants to splash some water on her face—mirror's shifting side to side she's drunk, has a laugh, there's a man—

He took a handful of her hair and smacked her face into the mirror—her forehead splits open on the impact, blood everywhere. It's a tiny fucking bathroom and it's only two bodies that fucking fit in there and he's between her and the door and the sink this fucking prick who just smashes and smashes and smashes the face of the woman I love into a mirror before he—

He—

I'm upstairs. Drink. Place is rammed. Drink. Solicitor talking to me about his wife. Blair, politics. At Chambers.

Where's Evie?

SCENE 5

The bedroom at Tom's mum's house in Wales. It's the middle of the night.

EVE *sits bolt upright in bed and gasps.*

EVE: I had a dream that we broke up. It was awful—the most awful thing—
TOM: You were screaming because we broke up.
EVE: [*laughing, relieved*] It was fucking horrible.

> TOM *also starts to laugh.*

There was this girl, this evil girl in your flat—and this staircase, this dark staircase going into dark—don't laugh at me. You wanted to go to the SupaSave and broke up with me—
TOM: Because you wouldn't let me go to the SupaSave?
EVE: This stupid staircase and I couldn't get out of this dream.
　　I couldn't get out of the dream.

　　Black.

Meal

CHARACTERS

    EVE, 30s
    TOM, 30s
    MANPREET, 27

SCENE

    Tom's flat in Kilburn, London.

TIME

    Meal takes place one year after *Muff* and six years after *Trip*.

PROLOGUE

MANPREET, EVE and TOM *play out a speed-dating event.*

MANPREET: I'm Manpreet, I'm twenty-eight. I've lived in London all my life. I work in the independent music industry as an event promoter. I'm up for a laugh, game for anything, I wear a lot of black and I've got a pierced clit.

TOM: I'm Tom, I'm not in my twenties anymore. I live in Kilburn and I run a venue circuit in London—one of them's the Green Note, you may have heard of it. You haven't heard of it? It's a venue, and I run it. I have a BA from the University of Sheffield.

MANPREET: I've got a degree, too—I should have mentioned that. In Psychology. Yeah, I know.

EVE: I'm Eve, I have a Masters in Education. I'm an English teacher. I taught in Tianming, in China, for three years. I can't remember my Chinese name. Being back in London does that to you.

A bell sounds.

MANPREET: I want to meet a guy who wants to fuck me loads.

TOM: I want to have a good time.

EVE: I want—something new.

Another bell sounds.

MANPREET: You could say I'm the type of girl who just can't say no. Name it, I've done it, and if I haven't heard of it I'll give it a go. Base jumping in Yosemite. I own my own skateboard. Group sex, acid. My heroes would be Marc Bolan, Keith Moon and the Manson Family.

TOM: Everyone's a product of their family environment. My father left us when I was ten. My sister is two years younger than I am and she had some rough years. I've taken my role as a protector very seriously.

EVE: I think scars are really attractive. It's something that's only occurred to me since I started going out again. I had a blind date with this Irishman recently and he kept touching his forehead— / [*Simultaneously, competing*] He was doing it all night and finally I said, 'Are you trying to—hide something?' and his hand just dropped to the table and he looked so sad and said that he'd been hurt playing basketball and he had this scar on his forehead; it wasn't that big but it was still red and he was so embarrassed.

MANPREET: [*simultaneous, competing*] / I love independent musicians. Usually drummers, half my luck. Seriously, though, there's so much talent in the undergrowth. I don't play anything myself—did piano until Year Five but not past that. Best gig I ever went to was The Libertines at Leeds Union. I love dancing.

TOM: [*simultaneously, competing*] / These days I'm more relaxed. When my—my major relationship ended—I went on holiday to Portugal, Spain, Gran Canarias. Took a couple of months out to—you can see the result. Nothing bothers me in the way it might have done. Running a venue chain's not where I saw myself going, but I'm doing well with the opportunity to expand.

MANPREET: Do you like my tongue stud?

TOM: These trainers are new. I like—to keep ahead of the brands.

EVE: I hadn't thought much of him until that moment when he went from being ordinary to being this—this story, this history ... It's like, people are a book, with one page. And every scar adds another page.

    I wanted to lick that scar all night.

    I'm going to have another drink. Would you like one?

A bell rings. EVE *disappears.* MANPREET *dons an apron.*

SCENE 1

Tom's flat in Kilburn. A dining table is out.

MANPREET: That will be her.

TOM: You're so excited.

MANPREET: I hope we've got enough enchiladas—

TOM: Enough *tortillas*.

MANPREET: Whatever.

    She screams.

Coming! [*To* TOM] Are you getting the door or standing here like a cockmonkey?

TOM: [*pressing a buzzer on the wall, calling out*] It's open!

> MANPREET *gives an excited squeal.* TOM *busies himself opening a bottle of wine.*
>
> EVE *enters. She's wearing a stylish coat.*
>
> MANPREET *runs over and gives her a hug.*

EVE: Hello, hello, you're excited.
TOM: Like a kitten on crack.
MANPREET: Check it out!
EVE: Hi.
TOM: Welcome to the palace.

> MANPREET *gives* EVE *a big kiss on the face.*

MANPREET: Ignore him and just look at my fucking house, bitch!
EVE: [*looking at the room*] Wow—when did all this happen?
MANPREET: Two weeks, go to whoa.
EVE: And all the bookshelves, too—you—
MANPREET: Tom is a real man's man. As it turned out. Massive surprise to me.
EVE: To everyone.

> *The bottle is uncorked.*

[*Producing a paper bag with a bottle of wine in it*] Before I forget. It's a South African pinot noir.
TOM: [*of his bottle*] So's this.
MANPREET: You didn't have to do that, Evie. That being said, I'm glad you did because I'm gonna drink it, certainly. You look hot in the trench, mate.
EVE: I've been pushing my style horizons. [*Of the apron*] As have you.
MANPREET: Fetish-wear. These *are* the best bookshelves in London—
TOM: —in England—
MANPREET: —in the world, in history—and we are celebrating because I just got a fucking cool new job.
EVE: Doing what?
MANPREET: I've been asked to organise the annual Voice of Slavery benefit. It's a charity that campaigns against modern slavery, there are *loads* of bands signed up to it already and it's the biggest gig I've ever done—
TOM: And hopefully it'll lead to bigger things.

MANPREET: And we're having enchiladas for dinner!
EVE: Congratulations.
MANPREET: You really like what we've done to the flat? I got all these plants from my dad—
EVE: A complete transformation.
MANPREET: Bet you wish you could move back in, then. Admit it.
EVE: Have you done anything with Ben's old room?
MANPREET: The spare room.
TOM: Your old room.
MANPREET: Look at the kitchen!
EVE: [*giving it a glance*] All very impressive …
MANPREET: We've got the last of the junk downstairs, but I'm on his back—aren't I?—I'm on his back to give the old shirts and socks to charity so some poor children in North London can be badly dressed—
TOM: Still enjoying Pimlico?
EVE: Central London is great. Walk everywhere.
MANPREET: You didn't walk here, did you? You didn't!
EVE: No. This wine—
MANPREET: I like a merlot but he said—Tom?—he / said—
TOM: / We used to drink a lot of it, when Eve was over—
MANPREET: When she lived here—
EVE: When—

> *An oven bell sounds.*

MANPREET: [*running out to attend to the oven*] Shit!
EVE: Can I see the room downstairs?
TOM: Eve—
EVE: What's wrong?
TOM: She's excited you're here.
EVE: I know. We talk.
TOM: You what?
EVE: Phone. One another.
TOM: When?
EVE: Tom, she knows about us. She's always known. Stop treating her like an idiot.

> *Beat.*

TOM: You can't see the room.

EVE: 'My old room'.
TOM: We're not going into places we both don't want to revisit—
EVE: Just South African pinot noir?
TOM: You bought the same bottle.
EVE: Because it amused me.
TOM: Let me help you with your coat.

> *He helps her to remove it. Underneath,* EVE *is dressed to go out—and dressed to pick up.* TOM *is gobsmacked.*
>
> MANPREET *comes back in.*

MANPREET: Fuck me, Evie—you look *gorgeous*. Were you planning to fuck both of us later?—because I am certainly up for it now!
EVE: I had plans to go out after dinner—but if you're on the table, I may reconsider.
MANPREET: I'd be on the table in a second to get my snorkel up that outfit. Doesn't she look hot, Tom?
TOM: She looks very lovely.
MANPREET: I haven't worn a dress like that in ages. Where would I wear it? Round our sitting room with the duster? While I'm cleaning the bath?
TOM: We know that'll never happen.
MANPREET: Cheeky. He only makes fun of me because he doesn't fuck me anymore. You move in together thinking it'll be cock on tap— you put up bookshelves and their dicks fall off, don't they, Tommy? You ever lived with a guy, Evie?
EVE: Not really.
MANPREET: It's funny learning to live with someone. You think you know everything but a *domestic setting* makes it all completely different.
EVE: You're enjoying it, then?
MANPREET: We're at that stage, you know. Put down the pills and the spliffs and the one-night stands, buy the flat and join Thomas here becoming a boring old fart. There's so many rules.
EVE: Rules?
MANPREET: I'm bringing this up, for confirmation, right? / You used to live here—
TOM: / Baby / —
EVE: / Baby—? [*To* MANPREET] Yes …

TOM: Here we go—
MANPREET: Is there a correct way to set the bog roll?
EVE: What?
MANPREET: Is there / —don't interrupt me, Daddy—is there, right, a particular direction that the bog roll needs to roll?
TOM: / Manpreet, is this really—?
EVE: I have no idea.
MANPREET: [*to* TOM] Ha!
TOM: How we choose to hang our bog roll is—
MANPREET: You're making up rules to oppress me, man!
EVE: What are you talking about?
MANPREET: He says— [*To* TOM] Shut it. [*To* EVE] He says that the paper's got to roll under the bar—it's the most ridiculous—and he needles me about it—about setting the fucking bog roll and it's not the least of what—there are rules—hanging the tea towels and washing the recycling bottles—he wasn't like this with you?
EVE: I think it's different if you're a couple, rather than just living together—
MANPREET: It should be just the fucking same! I can't believe this!
TOM: What Manpreet neglects to mention, Eve, is the utter filth she lived in. / Clothes instead of carpet. Mould on the walls. Eight kinds of crust in the bathroom.
MANPREET: / This is a fairy story. This is snuffafuckinglupaguss.
EVE: You used to live in a house in Sheffield that was ten times worse.
TOM: This wasn't a share house full of students. This was grown-up Manpreet—and her ex—cohabiting in filth.
MANPREET: Fuck off.
EVE: What I think is the more interesting part of the story is why you had such intimate knowledge of Manpreet's home when she was living with someone else.
MANPREET: Exactly. Exactly! Fess up. [*All over him*] He'd wanta rip my clothes off if I was the filthiest bitch alive. [*To him*] If I was naked in a pile of shit you'd cock right through. [*To both of them*] We fucked on those piles of clothes on the floor—and he loved it. We had sex in the bath so many times you'd have the crust under your fingernails. God, my stepmum's all about rules and charts and shit. Living with her was like living in an army barracks. We were alright, my sister

and my dad and me, and she moved in with alarm clocks and to-do lists … I hated it! My sister hated it. She—get this, right—my sister put this chart up in the toilet—this was to take the piss out of Merinda—and we had to write how many poos we'd done and Dad thought it was hilarious and Merinda's head nearly exploded—

The oven bell rings again. MANPREET *goes out.*

TOM *and* EVE *sit in the sitting-room. They are silent, but not frozen.*

TOM: Where are you going out?

EVE: [*laughing*] Is this what you expected of domestic bliss, Tom? Not only will she fuck you in a filthy bathtub and fill in a poo chart, but she'll tell the guests about it over dinner.

TOM: Stop it—

EVE: And you'd cock right through? You'd just cock right through.

TOM: Eve, please—

EVE: Nice house.

I'm looking forward to my enchiladas.

TOM: [*of the dress*] This isn't for me, is it?

EVE: Why can't I see my old room?

Are you turning it into a nursery?

TOM: She's not pregnant.

EVE: Are you planning—?

TOM: No!

EVE: Whose idea was moving in together?

TOM: It was something that happened. / It is an expected evolution / in a long-term relationship—

EVE: / Bullshit. / Someone who's a filthy little slut with a / filthy bathroom—

TOM: / Go down there. Go the fuck down there. You're so fucking curious, there's the fucking staircase / —

EVE: / You're clearly not comfortable with me intruding here and I should go.

TOM: *What are you fucking wearing here?!*

Pause.

If you're going to laugh at us, you shouldn't have come.

EVE: I'm not laughing at both of you.
TOM: Believe it or not—she actually really likes / you.
EVE: / Yes. She's made me feel very welcome.
TOM: Why can't you just fucking like her?!
EVE: I do. Listen to me: I—do.
TOM: She's my fucking girlfriend, get over it.
EVE: Who *you've* never said a word to, about me or you or us or anything!
TOM: [*hearing* MANPREET *approaching*] Pretend you've got a headache. I'll drive you home.

> MANPREET *comes back in again.* EVE *wipes tears of laughter from her eyes.*

MANPREET: [*to* EVE] What's wrong, Eve? You alright?
EVE: You're cooking onions.
MANPREET: You're that sensitive to onions?
TOM: We've probably gotten used to it.
MANPREET: Jesus, Evie, you look suicidal!

> *She laughs.*

I'll go and put the fan on. Don't kill yourself!
EVE: Tears of laughter, Manpreet. I promise.
MANPREET: Right, she's laughing, meaning she's not dead, meaning our first dinner party in the refurbed house—is an unqualified success.

> *She applauds and cheers.*

The dinner is progressing nicely, so I will now get drunk.

> TOM *pours* MANPREET *a wine.*

TOM: South African pinot noir.
EVE: It brings back a lot of memories.
TOM: We've been through some bottles of this.
EVE: I was surprised that they were still stocking it.
TOM: You didn't get this from the SupaSave—

> *She did.* TOM *and* EVE *laugh.*

MANPREET: Have your private little gags—it still tastes like squirrel piss.
TOM: [*to* EVE] She starts on the squirrel piss—you may get a word in. Talk quickly—she'll be under the table in five minutes.
MANPREET: How's work, Evie?

EVE: Work's work. The kids are—interesting. I enjoyed it at first but it's wearing on me now. It takes a special kind of person.
MANPREET: You're special. Who says you're not special?
EVE: I haven't got the patience for special needs kids.
MANPREET: They're not—they're not retarded—
EVE: They're EBD—
MANPREET: They're mentals.
TOM: Mentals as opposed to retards.
EVE: Mentals as opposed to retards, but in some ways that's more demanding. Not really mentals—abused, mostly. Bad homes, parents with absolutely no idea. You learn a lot about parenting working in those schools. Most of the parents are just kids themselves. One—my age, she's got six kids, four different fathers, the eldest kid is sixteen. I met her and thought she was even younger than she was. She had pink stickers on her mobile phone. There I was thinking, 'Love, Reiss is sixteen with a criminal record, you've got two more who are in and out of this place and three more under ten, you have more important things to do than put stickers on your mobile phone'.
MANPREET: Maybe she just got it like that, but. It could have been somebody else's.
TOM: I don't think that's really Eve's point.
EVE: There are better examples—
MANPREET: Six kids, no money, maybe her only outlet's putting stickers on her phone, you never know.
EVE: Maybe.
TOM: Manpreet, Jesus.
MANPREET: I'm just saying! Don't judge her!
EVE: All these situations are very complicated. / —Tom, let it drop.
TOM: / Eve works with these people every day—
MANPREET: She does, you don't.
TOM: Don't think this is personal, Eve—this is typical of Manpreet.
MANPREET: How am I typical?
TOM: You may think it's rude, / but it's some kind of psychological compulsion to argue with everyone. /
MANPREET: / How am I being rude? / I'm entitled to hold an opinion—I've worked with people like that, too—
TOM: You have?

MANPREET: There's always a lot more going on—there's more going on between us than anyone can see and that doesn't / mean—
EVE: / I was probably being too simplistic, Manpreet. I'm sorry if you—
MANPREET: See? Eve's willing to engage with what I'm saying and you should be, too.
TOM: You're making everyone uncomfortable.
MANPREET: Don't speak to me that way!

    Silence.

EVE: In other news, I've been going speed-dating.
TOM: What?
MANPREET: Really? That's awesome!
EVE: It's been a lot of fun.
TOM: What are you doing, going speed-dating?
MANPREET: What do you think she's doing? Look at her. [*To* EVE] Have you met anyone?
EVE: Yes.
MANPREET: Have you had any action?
TOM: Manpreet—
EVE: Yes. Loads. Enormous amounts.
    I used to—before China—I'd call myself frigid—
MANPREET: Steady on, Evie—!
EVE: [*she will not be interrupted*] You grow up with my well-meaning family, reading the magazines that tell you to wait, tell you it should be special and go into relationships, be in love—when that all falls apart you shag strangers for someone to talk to and the whole time—even in China, all those men—and it was never as good as masturbation. [*To* MANPREET] Coming back, meeting you: you're switched on, onto it, filthy, fucking filthy and proud—to go out and not think about, piss about—fucking *get some*—not for love, home, house, company, comfort—
MANPREET: At speed-dating?
TOM: To sit in a circle, learning in two minutes why not to fuck a merchant banker.
EVE: I fucked the living shit out of a merchant banker last week.
MANPREET: Way to go, Evie!
TOM: Well, I'm really looking forward to my enchiladas.
MANPREET: *Tortillas*, cockmonkey.

EVE: We've all known one another for years. I've heard you fuck, Tom—everything you do in this house. [*To* MANPREET] I've fucked lawyers and doctors and clerks and men from the council and huge fucking squaddies with dirty hands and firemen and chefs and a session guitarist who nearly bit my ear off and a shopgirl from Tesco whose cunt I could have stayed in for hours—
TOM: You don't do things like that—
EVE: Yes I do.
TOM: Manpreet, go and check on dinner.
MANPREET: Fuck dinner—this is much more entertaining. Tell me more about the shopgirl.
TOM: You're making Eve—
MANPREET: Crap I'm making Eve / anything—
TOM: / This is making *me* uncomfortable—can we stop?!
MANPREET: Calm down!
EVE: I never realised how much getting off is about enjoying control.

    I've shoved the heel of my shoe into a begging man's arsehole and heard him cry—
TOM: That's enough.
MANPREET: That's usually more than enough, and never enough, darling.
TOM: Go and check on dinner.
EVE: Come on, Tom—we're alright—
TOM: It's not alright, it's going to burn.
MANPREET: Will you chill the fuck out?!
TOM: Stop arguing with me and *check the fucking dinner*!

    MANPREET *leaves.*

You need help, Evie. You need to get back to the shrink and sort this all out. This behaviour's clearly some kind of pathology—
EVE: Having sex is pathology?
TOM: It's the rape, you're still recovering—
EVE: You're the one who's still recovering.
TOM: Bisexual and—what—fuck, Eve—that shrink you had—

    EVE *drinks wine.*

Is it true? Shoe heels and—?
EVE: Are you still tying her up? Still fucking her as hard as you can because you don't care / if you hurt her—?

TOM: / That's not what I said and that was a long time ago.

EVE: Not that long.

TOM: Tell me if it's true!

EVE: Whether it's true or not it's clearly turning you on.

TOM: Did you come here to torture me?!

EVE: I came because you invited me. Not Manpreet. You.

TOM: Yes, the downstairs room will be a nursery. It's going to be one, one day, obviously not yet. I'm thirty-four. I am thirty-four and I have a good job that's turning into a good career and there are things I want to do and—she's young and fun and—

EVE: —completely impossible not to like.

TOM: You'll meet someone, Eve. You will. I'm happy. I've made some tough decisions, but I—

EVE: You're so fucking stupid, Tom.

TOM: This was her idea.

EVE: Bollocks it was.

TOM: This was her idea and I let her go through with it and I should have stopped it and I didn't and now we're all / fucking uncomfortable.

EVE: Pot plants and bookshelves—aprons and corkscrews and the little woman in the kitchen. Why wouldn't I dress up for this? We're celebrating! It's a public vindication of *everything* you have that I don't.

TOM: I thought you were lonely. Not fucking merchant bankers and shopgirls like some kind / of—

EVE: [*screaming*] / You're turning my room into a nursery!

Oh, you must really be getting off now—a bit of suburban bondage could hardly compete with this—get your fist—get your damn fist, take a fat handful of my hair and smack my face into the mirror as hard as you can. Don't stop till it breaks, Tom! Don't stop till I'm bleeding all over you!

TOM: Is this what you want?

He grabs her by the hair, dragging her across the room.

Are you happy now?! Are you fucking happy yet?!

Horror.

He relents. His hands drop.

Horror.

MANPREET *comes back into the room in her kitchen apron, alerted by the noise.*

MANPREET: Why the fuck is everyone shouting?

Silence.

Tom?!

The oven bell howls.

END

MinusOneSister

Anna Barnes

Anna Barnes is an award-winning playwright and author. Her writing has been published in *Kill Your Darlings*, *Killings*, *The Lifted Brow* and the *Age*. Her book, *Girl! The Ultimate Guide To Being You* (Penguin 2012), was named one of the 2013 Eva Pownall Notable Books by the Children's Book Council of Australia.

Her plays and monologues have been performed around Australia. In 2007, she was the winner of the British Council's Realise Your Dream award, allowing her to go and study playwriting at Royal Court Theatre, London, UK. In 2012, she collaborated with comic artist Sara Drake (USA) to tell the story of losing her sense of smell for Radio with Pictures at the Sydney Opera House. She won Sydney Theatre Company's Patrick White Playwright's Award in 2013. Her play, *MinusOneSister*, opened at Griffin Theatre in October 2015, produced by Stories Like These for Griffin Independent.

MinusOneSister was first produced by Stories Like These as part of Griffin Independent at SBW Stables Theatre, Sydney, on 9 September 2015, with the following cast:

ELECTRA	Kate Cheel
IPHIGENIA	Lucy Heffernan
ORESTES	Liam Nunan
CHRYSOTHEMIS	Contessa Treffone

Director, Luke Rogers
Set and Costume Designer, Georgia Hopkins
Lighting Designer, Sian James-Holland
Sound Designer and Composer, Nate Edmondson
Stage Manager, Angharad Lindley
Producer, Peter Gahan

CHARACTERS

    CHRYSOTHEMIS
    ELECTRA
    ORESTES

WRITER'S NOTE

Unattributed lines are delivered by any of the actors playing a member of the chorus.

A slash (/) is an interruption point. If it appears after a line, it means you need to jump on this cue.

Gaps on a page are a rough approximation of silence.

If performed outside Melbourne (Australia) all geographic/advertisement references should be changed to reflect the city where the play is performed.

MinusOneSister was inspired by the play *Electra* by Sophocles.

0. THE MINUS ONE SISTER

- The last time you saw your minus one sister you were / watching tellie
- You were playing a game
- You were playing a game watching tellie
- Ads
- That was the game
- The first / person
- The first person to yell out the correct name of the company advertising wins
- The company not product
- Kraft not Vegemite
- Hungry Jacks
- Not Whopper
- Your sister
- Your minus one sister?
- Is very very good at this game
- Honda!
- There are some /
- Lean Cuisine!
- Some people who have a talent at /
- ANZ!
- Spelling say, or arithmetic
- No-one says / arithmetic anymore
- Slim Ease!
- But okay, well Maths, or maybe computers or basketball or cobbling or MS read-a-thon
- She was
- She was very very good at this game
- Ads
- You were losing
- You were playing
- You
- Your sister
- Minus one sister

- Bendigo Bank!
- And then your dad's assistant came in
- Which in retrospect
- In retrospect it was kind of weird cos your dad was away
- And
- And it was weird for the assistant to be there without him
- But he
- He came in and told you all that your sister had to go
- Go with
- Him
- And you were kinda happy
- 'Your mum's not in, is she?'
- Nuh
- Kinda
- Happy cos she was beating you
- Ads
- And you were a bit
- Well, sick of her
- School hols felt long when there were no parents to annoy
- But then maybe
- Yes maybe
- A bit resentful
- Resenting
- A bit
- Cos she was asked to go /
- And not you
- With Dad's assistant who so weirdly was now in the lounge room
- Like usual
- And she left
- Just
- Like
- That
- Minus one sister
- The worst things happen
- In the ad breaks
- When you're not paying attention

1. IN THE BEGINNING

- We
- You
- We were a family
- One
- Two
- Three
- Four
- Five
- And sitting
- Six
- And sitting
- Yes look at us all sit
- The pretty one
- The smart one
- The wild one
- The baby CEO
- Back for a meal
- Fadduh home
- Happy
- Happy cos work went well
- And he was back
- Back for a meal
- Everyone at their correct spot
- One
- Two
- Three
- Four
- Five
- And
- Six

2. IMAGE OF ELECTRA AND A HOSPITAL BED

ELECTRA *has just arrived at the mental clinic. She sits on a bed and puts her bag on the ground. As she sits, the bed rolls (it's on wheels) and she reaches down and pulls the wheel brake on. This is not her first rodeo.*

3. SLEEP HEAVY, PRINCESS

- If you could save a thousand lives by sacrificing / one
- Killing
- Would you not be immoral to sacrifice / the one?
- Killing
- No matter who they are
- To you
- No matter what their age
- Kill
- Their gender
- Kill
- Their race
- Kill
- Their standing
- But that is why he is such a good
- Leader
- Man
- He knew that
- He saw that
- He learnt that
- Early on
- Growing up
- In the public eye
- Sometimes
- You have to sacrifice the something you love
- To save everything you don't
- And he did
- He saved us
- Us
- And
- And it was hard for him
- The dad
- You could see it
- Their boss
- In his face
- After

- In his face
- After
- And the growing grey strip in the middle of his hair
- You could see it
- It was hard for him
- To sleep
- After
- After he did what he did
- To her
- His firstborn
- Hard
- Her
- But
- But while he couldn't sleep
- He knew he was right
- To do
- What he did
- Did
- Dad
- To her
- Because there / were no options
- There were no options
- But yes
- Yes the knowledge of killing his own daughter
- Didn't help him fall asleep
- Despite the lives he saved
- The funerals he avoided
- The cancelled mobile phone accounts
- The missing parent at parent-teacher interviews
- He still missed his daughter
- He was a man
- But he was a king
- A king among men
- He had no options
- The soldiers steered clear
- Knowing their lives were the cause
- Of the growing grey strip

- And the silent resentment you get / when you owe someone something
- And the silent resentment you get when you owe someone something
- He kept to himself
- He kept to himself when they were off the clock
- After
- No raiding of the bars
- After
- The battles
- The brothels
- Even when
- Even when they'd had a particularly good day
- In the rather average war
- Even then
- No cigars for Mr Clinton
- It was hard for him
- The dad
- Her dad
- Our boss
- But he knew he'd done the best
- For us
- For her
- His very best
- The men
- The soldiers outside the tent
- When they knew about the curse
- The need for blood
- To save their lives
- They fought to be the one that let the blood free
- Fifteen-year-old
- Schoolgirl
- Or not
- She had to die
- But he had arranged it first
- To avoid the careless chatter
- The clambering of limbs

- To twist the knife
- Into his own heart
- He got his assistant
- His best friend
- To do it
- She was asleep
- She didn't feel a thing
- Off to the angry god
- That requested her death
- God works in mysterious ways
- And that's how we do it in the NBA
- Sleep was for fools anyway
- Clinton slept two hours a night when he was in the White House
- Tesla
- Napoleon
- Martha Stewart
- All less than four hours
- Plus it gave him more time to plan
- And that's what he was here for
- Only a few more years
- And this war will be over?
- Yes
- And then I will return to my wife
- Yes
- Her
- She
- And my girls and
- He
- And everything will be okay
- Then I will be able to sleep

4. OUR GIRLS

- A house of girls and only one boy
- Only one boy?
- Lining up
- Sisters

- One
- Two
- Three
- Two years apart
- One
- Two
- Years apart
- Perfect separation
- Separation of such perfection to allow
- To allow own friends
- Own classes
- Own clothes
- Own boyfriends
- To avoid
- Crossovers
- Clashes
- Crashes
- Two years and look at them line up
- One
- Two
- Three
- And in that order too
- The smart one
- The pretty one
- The wild one
- Wild?
- Has panache
- A nightmare to tame
- A fortune in therapy bills
- But the favourite nonetheless
- And then the brother
- Look at him go
- Little bow tie
- Mr CEO
- Baby CEO of Baby Co Limited
- Incorporated
- Look at him grow

- But
- Yes, but even despite the careful
- The perfect
- Yes the perfect separation
- You know how girls are
- Well the differences were perhaps?
- Too
- Much?
- Too
- Stark?
- The pretty one
- Just too pretty
- The smart /
- So much smarter than the others
- And the wild—well
- Yes
- Yes
- Took right after her father
- A girl CEO
- Almost
- Almost exactly like her father—but
- No
- No
- Childish issues
- Girls
- Girlish fissures
- A house of girls and only one boy
- Only one boy
- And you know how relentless
- Tension
- Jealousy
- Gossip
- Pressure
- So much pressure these days
- Texting
- Sexting
- Internets

- Trolls
- 'Glee'
- So much pressure these days
- And with no release
- Princess Bitchface
- She just turns into
- As if
- As if no-one else has / ever before
- As if no-one else has ever before
- But completely normal
- Normal
- Girlish fissures
- With no release
- Father always away
- Brother so young
- No masculine presence
- Pleasance
- A house of girls and only one boy
- And you know how / girls get
- You know how girls get

5. THE VISIT

- A bed
- White
- Bright
- 'This is nice.'

ELECTRA: The mother said
- 'So the nurse said you're settling …'

ELECTRA: The mother said
- 'You look better.'

ELECTRA: The mother said
- '(This place) is the best there is …'

ELECTRA: The mother / said
- 'Expensive.'

ELECTRA: The mo / ther
- 'Worth every penny.'
- 'For you.'

- The mother said
- 'Say something for heaven's sake.'
ELECTRA: Fuck you cunt
- 'That, that is great, that's just …'

6. PLAIN AS A PICTURE

- There was this girl
- No, woman
- No
- Sorry
- There was this princess
- I went to school with her
- She was a year above me
- No, below me
- A year above me
- And
- And she had two sisters
- So sorry there was three girls /

Kate Cheel as Electra in Griffin Independent's 2015 production of MinusOneSister *in Sydney. (Photo: Brett Boardman)*

- Princesses, and they were pretty happy
- They were good at school and stuff
- House captains and
- Did stuff like spoke at assembly
- Raised money for disabled people and horses
- And um, then one of them had to go away for a bit
- Just overseas
- Or something and so her dad had this
- Sorry, her dad
- Her dad was a really big deal
- A king
- Among men
- And she was actually
- She was actually going overseas to see her dad
- He was away a lot
- And sometimes he'd fly his family out to meet him you know?
- Just fly them out, cos
- Cos it was easier for him to do that
- Than to get time off work
- Cos he was like kinda
- Really
- Big
- Deal
- So anyway, he decided to get her to come out
- To fly out to meet him
- His daughter
- He said it would be like a really good opportunity for her
- Going to see
- To meet, and
- It didn't really matter cos the principal would always let her go
- She always did
- His name was on the new wing of the library
- The dad's name
- Anyway, so because she was young
- A year below me at school, he got his assistant to pick her up and fly with her on the plane
- Stranger danger and all that jazz

- Even though
- Even though, these days it's a bit better
- These days you can tell the flight attendants or something
- Like with food
- Like a vegan
- Like a vegan exactly
- You can tell them that it's a minor and they will take extra special care of you
- Like a vegan
- But they didn't tell the attendants
- They had the assistant fly with her instead
- Anyway, when they were on the plane the assistant, the dad's assistant, started to creep onto her, his boss's daughter. You know, you can just feel it, eyes, looks too long and she was stuck on this plane just turning up her earphones as if, as if the sound could get her out and he was putting his hand on her arm, where they shared the armrest, he had like his arm on hers and he kept looking at her. And this was a twenty-hour flight so this was a bit of a fucking problem for her. So there she is and she's got sixteen hours to go, and she can't fall asleep cos her dad's assistant is gonna do something bad and she's fucked. She is really uncomfortable, and she just thinks if she can keep herself awake and alert she can avert the whole thing, the whole thing when she tells her dad—the yelling, his, the crying, hers. Cos the assistant, the creepy dad's assistant had actually been with the family for a long time, since as long as she can remember he'd been there at the dinner table. So God knows how, she manages to stay awake and away from him the whole time, just back straight you know?
- Back straight
- Eyes ahead
- Music loud
- And so as they touch down, she's thinking sweet: home and free / …
- And also, she's also a bit excited cos she's going to see her dad, and she hasn't seen him in forever. She's excited that

he picked her, that out of the three girls, the three sisters, it was her name he requested, she's excited. So they get back to the hotel—they're going to the meet the dad for dinner after a nap—and she gets her key and says goodbye to creepy assistant of the dad. But as she opens her door …
- *Bam!*
- From behind he slams her head against the door, and then he, the creep, the dad's assistant, he turns the key and she falls inwards, face first into her room and he kicks her feet outta the way and locks the door behind him. So he drags his own boss's daughter into the bathroom while she's unconscious from the first hit, and he um, you know. And then he rapes her again on the bed when she's waking up with slow painful eyefuls and then he does it again against the hotel desk, just so she gets the message. Don't fucking make a sound, he says. Don't fucking make a sound and she starts to kinda breathe quick. It's not crying cos this is beyond tears but just kinda huff like the air is an asthma puffer and she can huff

From left: Liam Nunan as Orestes, Lucy Heffernan as Iphigenia and Kate Cheel as Electra in Griffin Independent's 2015 production of MinusOneSister *in Sydney. (Photo: Brett Boardman)*

puff herself away from this man, this room, this fucking night and she sort of crumples in on herself like an inwards sneeze and she lets herself fall because she can't seem to be able to stand anymore.
- To stand
- To breathe
- To move
- Has been lost
- She's gone
- So when they get back home
- The king
- The dad
- The kinda big deal
- Without his daughter
- She's gone
- He gets home and he is made out as some kinda hero, some fucking war hero. Cos he sacrificed his own and then the powers that be were happy to let the men
- His men
- Our men
- Go safe. Home to their wives, their daughters, their baby CEOs, home to their bathrooms, their beds and their hotel desks. Safe
- I went to school with her
- She was a year below me
- Above me
- She was a year below me

7. TWO, NO THREE, NO TWO SISTERS

- Two sisters plaiting hair
- Three
- Two sisters plaiting hair
- There were three sisters
- No, three minus one, two sisters
- Plaiting
- Hair

- Perhaps or whatever young girls do on a winter's night waiting for their dad to get home
- Dinner—bakedies and toast soldiers all eaten
- Even crusts?
- All eaten
- And waiting in the front room
- Tellie on, but no-one is watching, it is / beside the point
- Background
- Yes, it's on in the background
- Mother in the kitchen
- Like the tellie, there-but-not
- But not
- Like the third sister?
- Exactly
- There-but-not
- And they're playing a game known only to them which in the retelling will seem clever and cute but in actuality is
- Neither
- A game just to pass the time
- Like a bottle of wine on a Monday evening between the vast emptiness of dinner and sleep
- Like a bottle of wine
- On a Monday evening
- Something to block out the background noise
- The there-but-nots
- The mother
- The tellie
- The sister
- There-but-nots
- He's late
- Running late
- Called from the airport
- His assistant maybe, called
- From the airport
- But he's here, there, he's nearly here
- And the two
- Three

- Two sisters are told to go to bed
- You'll see him in the morning
- Which
- 'Witch'
- Which is completely unfair
- You haven't seen him for
- *Forever*
- And he's at the airport
- But she
- The there-but-not
- The mother
- Sends you both upstairs
- One of you starts to cry
- Not you
- The other one
- Starts to cry
- But it doesn't matter
- Nothing really matters anymore
- Since the minus one sister
- 'Mum—'
- Bed
- 'Bed!'
- And you go upstairs, where you've been moved recently since / the
- Since the minus one sister, you have the room at the top of the stairs—her room
- Which is smaller than your old room but now you don't have to share with your brother anymore
- Your brother!
- The brother!
- How we forgot
- Where is your brother?
- Staying with family?
- At a school camp in Point Lonsdale?
- At some sort of extracurricular wind surfing tutorial weekend where the kids stay in apartment-style housing and call the teacher dude instead of miss or sir?

- Dude
- Exactly
- He is also—
- There-but-not
- So you now have your own room
- Which isn't as monumental as your mum thinks
- But that's because you're not old enough to be ashamed of yourself
- Yet
- To need privacy
- Yet
- To change under your doona in fear of hidden cameras streaming to the internet
- You're not old enough
- Yet
- Bedtime
- So you go to bed
- But the joke's on her
- Witch
- The joke's on her cos you go to bed
- You even brush your teeth but
- But you don't go to sleep
- You've got important business
- Important business
- You've been waiting for this day
- This morning
- This night when he returns
- You've been waiting forever and you have things to say
- Things you don't even know how to say
- Things you don't even know
- Except muffled voices
- Uncle here
- Uncle there
- Muffled voices
- You have important business
- You get under your doona and you wait

8. *A HORRIBLE TRIP*

CHRYSOTHEMIS: Tonight I had a horrible trip here. The train, and ticket rejected, and everyone looking at me, people behind, the people behind me pushing up against, as if this will help, will turn the red light, the continually red light turn green. And I just keep swiping my card against the swiper thing again and again—so I guess I'm like them—the people behind me, pushing, I guess I'm the same—continuing on, soldiering on. And then the sounds begin, people start sighing, not normal sighing, sighing to make a point. Sighing as if it's a word, like coughing. Like when you cough to get someone's attention, like when I coughed when I saw Mum, when I saw Mum in my room, the laundry basket still in her arms, my mum in my room crying. Cough. She had been crying. Cough. And she saw me, but it was if she didn't recognise me, she saw me but she didn't. 'He killed her, love, he killed your sister.' Cough. And the people behind me, the people at the station were sighing like that and someone said gruffly, 'Come on', gruffly. *Come on!* And then I started making noises too, in reaction to their noises. I started exhaling in despair, panic, enough panic in my voice to show—surprise and displeasure—to show that I wasn't doing this on purpose. And when that didn't seem to be sufficient, the exhaling in despair, the panic and surprise, the surprise and displeasure: 'This shouldn't be happening'. This shouldn't be happening and everyone kept pushing, and I was still there, red, the light was still red and I was looking for a man, an attendant, to come and help me. Come and open the gate, come and make the red light stop—because my card was charged, this shouldn't be happening. Weeks pass, every Tuesday morning, weekly, save five dollars and something cents and it was Thursday so I had four, no three, no four more days before this should be happening. This shouldn't be happening and so I was looking for an attendant to come and make it green, come make all of this go away.

    He killed your sister.

9. SMASH

- And later
- Later that night
- That night when your dad had come home
- Finally come home
- And you were waiting
- Under the doona
- Waiting
- Just when you had rested
- Just rested your eyes
- From the very important information
- He is there
- In the corner of the room
- In the dark
- Black night
- Head kissed
- Checked in on
- He is there
- In the corner of the room
- Kneeling
- Crying
- Crying as he is kneeling
- This is when you remember
- This was not your room
- When he left
- She left
- He is crying for
- Minus one sister
- You are still
- You don't want to make a
- You don't want to break
- The crying
- The dark
- Maybe it isn't him
- You think
- Maybe it's your brother

- Back from school camp
- But no
- No
- But
- 'Dad'
- Whisper loud
- 'Dad'
- Not so loud as to wake / her
- Her
- 'Dad'
- 'E?'
- Awake
- You
- I
- Should
- Am
- Be asleep
- Awake
- Girl
- Important business
- To share
- And he stands up
- Walks across
- Mum
- 'E?'
- 'Uncle here'
- 'Mum'
- 'Uncle there'
- You say
- Things you don't even know
- How to say
- Muffled voices
- Important
- Business
- But you've started now
- And you
- Can't

- Stop
- 'Uncle here'
- 'Mum'
- 'Uncle there'
- Muffled voices
- Important business
- He says nothing
- For
- One
- Two
- Three
- He leaves
- Smash
- The light
- The light under the door
- Thick
- Light
- Until he stepped into it
- To talk to her
- About uncle
- Muffled voices
- Important business
- And the light shattered
- It shattered like one of those fake crystal glasses / she kept on the liquor cabinet next to her brandy
- It shattered like one of those fake crystal glasses she kept on the liquor cabinet next to his brandy
- And when a light is shattered
- It is never the same / again
- Never the same again
- Dark room
- Girl minus father
- Shattered
- Never the same again

10. TWO SISTERS

CHRYSOTHEMIS *has come to visit* ELECTRA. *She has brought her Pantene ProV conditioner and shampoo.*

CHRYSOTHEMIS: You got a single room this time, how did you manage that one?
ELECTRA: Quick blowie to the head nurse and there you go, room with a view.
CHRYSOTHEMIS: Classy lady. I bought your conditioner.
ELECTRA: Thanks sister.
CHRYSOTHEMIS: Any frequent flyers in?
ELECTRA: Gianni from last year.
CHRYSOTHEMIS: Is he the one that constantly tells you he is being followed by ASIO?
ELECTRA: No that's Simon. Gianni is the one that closed down Myers with the fake sword.
CHRYSOTHEMIS: Oh yeah, the redhead.
ELECTRA: Other than that, it's a whole new ward.

> CHRYSOTHEMIS *and* ELECTRA *sing some lines from 'A Whole New World' (*Aladdin*).*

CHRYSOTHEMIS: So how long will this stint last?
ELECTRA: I'm not the one that chose to be here you know?
CHRYSOTHEMIS: You're awfully skinny.
ELECTRA: That has nothing to do with it.
CHRYSOTHEMIS: Dr Edmunds didn't have much choice but to admit you.
ELECTRA: Dr Edmunds does whatever Mum says.
CHRYSOTHEMIS: She just wants you to be better.
ELECTRA: Of course she does.
CHRYSOTHEMIS:
ELECTRA:
CHRYSOTHEMIS: It's bad for your hair, you know.
ELECTRA:
CHRYSOTHEMIS: It might look good, but my hairdresser said it's apparently like really bad for the hair. It puts like gasoline or glycerine or something so it looks shiny.

ELECTRA: I don't really care.
CHRYSOTHEMIS: Hairdressers hate it.
ELECTRA:
CHRYSOTHEMIS: You've got to get better, Electra. Please.
ELECTRA:
CHRYSOTHEMIS: I'm on your side.
ELECTRA: I know you are.
CHRYSOTHEMIS: I just.
ELECTRA: You just, exactly.
CHRYSOTHEMIS: What am I suppose to do then?
ELECTRA: Not answer to her beck and call. Have a backbone. Stop sticking up for her.
CHRYSOTHEMIS: I have a backbone.
ELECTRA: You live with them.
CHRYSOTHEMIS: Yeah and you live in a mental clinic.
ELECTRA: Rather that than have to deal with her manipulative crap.
CHRYSOTHEMIS: She, it's complicated.
ELECTRA: Will you ever fucking wake up to the fact our mum is a monster?
CHRYSOTHEMIS: It's been nine years.
ELECTRA: Ten.
CHRYSOTHEMIS: No, nine, no ten years. It's been years.
ELECTRA: Yeah you'd get less for murder, oh that's right she got … how much? Four months.
CHRYSOTHEMIS: What's the use of constantly bringing it up?
ELECTRA: What's the use? Oh, I don't know, justice?!
CHRYSOTHEMIS: You're such a drama queen.
ELECTRA: Bite me.
CHRYSOTHEMIS: You are not Aladdin, E, you are Jasmine. Put on some weight, stop acting like a fucking dick, and come home.

11. BOY MONDAYS

- It was hard to be a boy amongst so many girls
- Thought the dad
- His dad
- Their dad
- One

- Two
- Three
- Lining up
- His youngest child
- The rightful heir
- So much smaller than the rest
- Three girls
- Towering over him
- And him, running along after
- He loved his sisters
- And they loved him
- Spoiling him rotten and
- Baby CEO
- A human cat to dress up
- But the dad
- Their dad
- His dad
- Watched this
- With worry
- Because while the sisters adored their little brother
- Orestes
- They also adored Twisties
- And
- Free make-up that comes with magazines
- And McDonald's
- And new ballet shoes
- And lip balm that smelt like watermelon
- And Orestes could not keep up
- He wanted their full attention
- All the time
- But
- Twisties
- Free make-up /
- He could not compete
- His existence was of interest to his sisters
- But only when there was nothing else to distract them
- He was

- Show and tell
- On a slow day
- And as they got older
- And older
- And older
- This interest waned and
- Suddenly baby brother wasn't allowed in their room anymore
- Girls only
- And when he saw them in the playground
- Girls
- They no longer rushed to his side
- Only
- And plaited his hair
- You're too old for that O
- And the dad
- Their dad
- His dad watched this with worry
- He saw the crumpled face of his five-year-old
- The way he had recently become so quiet
- Sat by himself watching his sisters
- Talking to himself
- Mirroring their moves from across the room
- He'd been away for the raising of his daughters
- Fadduh
- Abroad
- Muddah
- At home
- But he was here now
- And he'd be damned if he watched his only boy become a sissy she-boy in his older sisters' skirts
- So he took charge
- He created Boys' Monday
- A night for him and the sissy boy to get out of the house of
- One
- Two
- Three
- Sisters

- And do boys' stuff
- On a Monday
- Boys' Monday

12. SCHOOLBOY

- After the death
- The murder
- The funeral
- Baby CEO was banished
- To a boarding school in Europe
- He shouldn't see the court case
- Muddah said
- But the sisters did
- Could
- And he was
- Young
- Almost
- Yes, almost too young
- To understand what it meant to have cameramen on your front lawn
- But the mother decided he needed space
- Authority
- Routine
- Plus there was the chance of jail time
- For mother
- And no-one wants their only son
- The rightful heir
- To see that
- She said
- The sisters listened to this
- The mother's explanation to the empty kitchen
- As if making a case
- To a roomful of mothers
- They knew this wasn't the case
- They knew
- The sisters

- —
- Two
- Three
- The remaining two
- They knew
- And even though
- Yes even though they loved him
- They too wished he would just disappear
- He was too young
- Too too young
- To be around
- He didn't understand
- —
- The police
- The ambulance
- The blood
- He didn't understand
- 'You fucking retard he's not coming back'
- It is hard for a child to know what this means
- He was used to his dad's absences
- The triumphant return
- The cab in the driveway
- The presents
- The hugs
- So while the idea of losing another
- So soon
- Was hard
- They couldn't be around him either
- So he went
- So young
- And his life became
- A boarder's life
- A military school
- Boarder's life
- For wayward children
- Of the elite
- And here he was

- Australian accent
- Too-big suit trousers
- And here in Europe
- Six years and five months and three days
- Old
- His suitcase was heavier than he
- But it wasn't all bad
- They have Mondays in Europe
- He thought
- That was lucky
- His first day
- Lucky he could still do Boys' Mondays
- In Europe

13. TAKING SIDES

CHRYSOTHEMIS *visits* ELECTRA *again.*

CHRYSOTHEMIS: The nurse said you're hiding food again.
ELECTRA: Hardly.
CHRYSOTHEMIS: They said you lost weight at weigh-in.
ELECTRA: Hardly anything.
CHRYSOTHEMIS: They said you are threatening Mum in your therapy.
ELECTRA: Are they allowed to tell you all this?
    Stephanie had a breakthrough in group today.
    She realised that her bulimia was to do with the abuse her dad suffered from his mum. That her bulimia was because of intergenerational trauma. How privileged is that shit? You don't even need to have your own trauma to get in here, you can borrow some off an ancestor.
CHRYSOTHEMIS:
ELECTRA: I offered her some of ours, I mean, we've got plenty to go around.
CHRYSOTHEMIS: I'm so tired, Electra.
ELECTRA: It's like those people that have tattoos of their dead pets. Seriously, that's the best thing you have to be sad about? To commemorate.

CHRYSOTHEMIS: Just stop.
ELECTRA: You right there? Having a moment are you, sister?
CHRYSOTHEMIS: I don't care about Stephanie.
ELECTRA: No-one does, that's her problem.
CHRYSOTHEMIS: This is the fifth time you've been in here this year.
ELECTRA: Yeah?
CHRYSOTHEMIS: What if you will never be normal again?
ELECTRA: Normal?
CHRYSOTHEMIS: You know what I mean.
ELECTRA: No, you're right, I will never be normal again.
CHRYSOTHEMIS: I feel, it makes me feel …
ELECTRA: Ohhh, 'I feel' sentences!
CHRYSOTHEMIS: Oh for fuck's sake, Electra, you can really be a sanctimonious bitch sometimes.
ELECTRA:
CHRYSOTHEMIS: I'm sorry. I'm just.
ELECTRA: Tired?
CHRYSOTHEMIS: Yes.
ELECTRA: Me too.
CHRYSOTHEMIS:
ELECTRA: You should try a spell in here. Really gets your sleeping habits back / in line.
CHRYSOTHEMIS: She was fourteen years old.

A sharp intake of breathe from the CHORUS.

ELECTRA:
CHRYSOTHEMIS: E, she was fourteen years old when he killed her. When we watched her get taken away.
ELECTRA:
CHRYSOTHEMIS: One
ELECTRA: Two
CHRYSOTHEMIS: Three
ELECTRA: Under the doona.
CHRYSOTHEMIS: Two little girls.
ELECTRA: Hiding from her.
CHRYSOTHEMIS: From him.
ELECTRA: She made us look like, like fucking—

CHRYSOTHEMIS:
ELECTRA: The 'abuse' and the, she made us all look—she lied.
CHRYSOTHEMIS: E, he killed her.
ELECTRA: He was an honourable man.
CHRYSOTHEMIS: He killed my big sister.
ELECTRA: We were an honourable family.
CHRYSOTHEMIS: Now?
ELECTRA: Now we're a fucking bunch of fiddled-with girls.

14. THE RECKONING

- The truth came out
- Like any other through a
- School project
- Where do you come from?
- A popular class for the Year Eights
- The school a dumping ground
- For kids in the way
- Had children from all over
- And after that suicide
- Of the Year Niner
- Cos of teasing of his accent
- The school board /
- The school board had decided to encourage the kids to understand where they were all coming from
- Tolerance with a grade
- So it became a school tradition
- The presentation of your family tree
- One
- Two
- Three
- So he wrote his family
- The boy
- No longer baby
- CEO
- Send me pics
- A sentence he was familiar with as a teenage boy
- Pics or it didn't happen

- But no reply
- It didn't happen
- He scoured Facebook for his sisters' profiles
- He had to sign up
- He had no Facebook
- But all teenage girls have Facebook
- Don't they?
- He couldn't find them
- So he was stuck
- Prospect of another lousy grade
- He was not a star pupil
- Like his sisters
- So
- He googled it
- A half-hearted attempt
- Hoping maybe his family name would bring up a history site
- Or an ancestor invented something?
- But no, just heaps of stories about some crazy murder years ago
- Photos of little girls with pigtails being marched into the courtroom
- —
- Two
- Three
- Screaming
- Headlines about
- Love and
- Revenge
- Death
- And
- Honour
- Murderous mother
- Abusive husband
- Divided community
- The boy skimmed
- And drummed along to the music playing from next door's dorm

- Until
- The recognition hit
- The blurry memory of an itchy suit
- A boring church service
- The flickering lights of cameras
- The recognition hit
- Like a bong pulled before first period in the science lab that the school doesn't use anymore
- He needed that first hit
- After the memories began to come back
- He kept the news articles in a folder on a flash drive
- No prying eyes
- Not that anyone would try
- Every boy has his secrets
- His family secrets
- And as awful as it sounded
- It made a lot of sense
- To him
- His parents not seeing him for Easter hols
- Summer hols
- Christmas hols
- Just him and Xiang, the boy from down the corridor, the only boys not going home for Christmas
- Picked up by a limo and driven to the hotel
- Happy Christmas Xiang
- The blurry memory of an itchy suit
- A boring church service
- The flickering lights of cameras
- The reckoning had begun

15. REPROACH OF HER ABSENCE

- The choice was made
- Not easy
- No
- Long time
- Agony
- Painful gasps of air

- You can see it
- Clear as a picture
- Her father
- Your father
- Standing in the boardroom
- His daughter's name on the whiteboard
- Clear as a picture
- The numbers were
- Undeniable
- She saw them
- After
- She saw them, and had to agree
- The savings far outweighed the
- Cost?
- But
- Your mum says no child should lose their lives
- Even to spare hundreds more
- But—
- You
- Electra has pause
- Surely
- Surely to save hundreds one cannot be saved
- No matter
- Who the family
- Who the daughter
- Who the beauty
- Electra has pause
- When you went back to school
- You and your sister
- Now minus one sister
- There was
- A quiet acceptance
- Amongst the girls
- Even her friends did not question her absence
- We all knew what had happened to her
- Without ceremony
- We all knew

- The Year Seven girls made a flowerbed memorial
- She was so pretty!
- And girls left cards and flowers on her locker
- She was so pretty!
- But no-one spoke
- The guilt of being saved
- The reproach of her absence
- Kept them all silent
- A silence bought
- By a debt weighed heavy
- But silence cannot last forever
- And the flowers on her metal locker
- Stuck with sticky tape
- Left without water
- Died
- And the memorial flowerbed was trampled on during one fire drill
- Until the plaque alone was left
- An empty square of dirt
- RIP
- And soon the talking began
- About two weeks later
- In hushed whispers
- Two weeks later
- By Home Economics rooms and
- Rollcall meetings
- Can you believe it?
- And one girl would say
- I knew it
- I could tell
- She had it written all over her face
- A Monday in PE
- She said
- About minus one sister
- All over her face
- She said
- And the photo

- The formal photo
- They'd used on the news
- Just added more to the
- Hushed whispers
- That dress
- Short and slutty
- Even for her
- Minus one sister
- And there were rumours that
- He called for her a lot
- That the father
- The dad
- Saw her beauty
- Too
- Little Lolita
- She made her moves on him
- Too
- Little Lolita
- And at the
- Boys' school across the way
- There were rumours that she gave
- One
- Two
- Three
- Boys head at a party one night
- All lined up
- In a row
- She was so pretty!
- One
- Two
- Three
- Wasted on Bacardi Breezers
- Wasted on her knees
- My boyfriend's brother
- Cousin's friend
- Brother's basketball teammate
- Was there

- The night
- Minus one sister
- Gave three guys head in a row
- And the guilt dissipated with each new story
- The guilt of being saved by someone
- You didn't even know
- Because
- She was so / pretty!
- She had it coming
- After all
- She had it coming
- The boys talked about her as if
- Intimately
- They knew her
- As if all of them had
- Received
- Knee-given presents
- Wink
- Wink
- They would mention her name
- And their girlfriends would
- Explode
- The silence
- With hatred
- And when things got nasty
- 'Hey lay off'
- 'Have some fucking respect'
- 'You girls would bite each other's heads off'
- 'If it wasn't for us'
- And the girlfriends
- Would nod
- But
- No
- Yes
- Nod
- No
- It would never be me
- She isn't like us

- Bitch
- Mother-fucking
- Slut
- He's not talking about me
- She put herself in a
- Stupid
- Situation
- The choice was hard
- Short
- And slutty
- But the aftermath was easy
- Even for her
- The minus one sister
- They're not talking about me
- They're not talking about me
- They're not talking about me

16. SATURN RETURNS

ORESTES *has come to visit* ELECTRA *on ward for the first time.*

ELECTRA: I can't believe you're here.
ORESTES: I sent you a message.
ELECTRA: I didn't get it.
ORESTES: On Facebook.
ELECTRA: We're not allowed computers on ward.
ORESTES: Oh.
ELECTRA: Or mobiles.
ORESTES: Serious?
ELECTRA: Cos pop the screen and slicey slicey.
ORESTES: Jesus.
ELECTRA: Life is dark. When did you come home, little brother?
ORESTES: So they just put you in here for no reason?
ELECTRA: She put me in here for no reason.
ORESTES: And him?
ELECTRA: Of course. Stepfather knows best.
ORESTES: You look …
ELECTRA: Like you?

ORESTES: Skinny.
ELECTRA: So what grade are you in now?
ORESTES: Are you okay?
ELECTRA: Yes. I'm fine. Just respite. All good. How did you get here?
ORESTES: Plane.
ELECTRA: No, I mean.
ORESTES: It's semester break. I just thought. It was time.
ELECTRA: Have you spoken to anyone else?
ORESTES: No. / Yes.
ELECTRA: Good.
ORESTES: Chrysothemis.
ELECTRA: And?
ORESTES: What?
ELECTRA: What did she say?
ORESTES: She told me you're here.
ELECTRA: And?
ORESTES: She told me visiting times were six to eight p.m. She told me to catch the two or the eight and get off at the Domain Interchange.
ELECTRA: And here you are. She's a smart one, isn't she?
ORESTES: She told me you tried to kill yourself.
ELECTRA: Of course she did.
ORESTES: Did you?
ELECTRA: No!
ORESTES: She said you don't eat.
ELECTRA: She has a lot to say, little brother. A lot to say about me, about her sister—but nothing to say about the fact she's living with a couple of murderers.
ORESTES: Yeah.
ELECTRA: Yeah.
ORESTES: She said she didn't want me to see you. She said it might bring up demons for you.
ELECTRA: Demons? Demon is the woman that stabbed our dad forty-three times, forty-three times and let him bleed to death on the floor of our bathroom while we are upstairs hiding under a fucking doona.
ORESTES: Mum?

ELECTRA: The very same. Oh, and of course her accomplice that we're supposed to call Dad.
ORESTES:
ELECTRA: It's so good to see you, Orestes.
ORESTES: It's. I didn't realise I had …
ELECTRA: All this craziness?
ORESTES: No.
ELECTRA: And she's proud of it, you know? Proud of what she did.
ORESTES:
ELECTRA: And the insinuation, the term, the word, 'abusive'.
ORESTES: Yes.
ELECTRA: As if, we all, as if he was a—
ORESTES: In all of the interviews.
ELECTRA: Open up the paper and there she was, there she is—smiling, proud of what she did. And people writing in, in support, people calling her a lioness. A lioness protecting her cubs.
ORESTES: And / the …
ELECTRA: But we're her cubs! We are the cubs and she isn't protecting us. She's crying about the dead daughter, the pretty one, she's crying about her and sleeping with that imposter in our dad's bed …
   I'm really glad you've come home, little brother.
ORESTES: So what are we going to do?

17. FLASHING LIGHTS

- You remember the sirens
- Or was it the screams first?
- The siren then scream, no, scream then siren
- The lights
- Flashing
- Into your window
- You are sitting on your bed again
- Under the doona
- Again
- Your sister is there
- Not the minus one sister
- Just you and your sister
- Waiting under the doona

- Again
- When you heard the first scream
- You were ready and waiting
- You had heard this before
- Muddah
- Fadduh
- He sometimes needed to
- Make a point
- Especially now
- You thought
- Especially now with the uncle
- Here
- There
- In your house
- In her bed
- Muffled voices
- Important Business
- He had to

Kate Cheel (left) as Electra and Contessa Treffone as Chrysothemis in Griffin Independent's 2015 production of MinusOneSister in Sydney. (Photo: Brett Boardman)

- Make a point
- With muddah
- But it wasn't her scream it was his
- It was his
- Fadduh
- And when you ran to the door
- You saw her
- Muddah
- You saw her with blood all over her
- His blood
- Fadduh
- It was his
- Then under the doona
- Then sirens
- Screams
- Now waiting
- And it seems like forever
- Waiting
- Under the doona
- One of you starts to cry
- Not you
- The other one
- Before you hear the steps of someone coming up to the room
- Your room
- Your minus one sister's old room
- A smiley policewoman
- Hand out
- Palms flat
- 'Come on, girls'
- Palms flat
- I'm not going to hurt you
- As if this is what we were hiding from
- As if she was what we were hiding from

18. MOTHER KNOWS BEST

- When your child is sick there are a number of things to look out for

- You can check them off a list
- Hot forehead
- Check
- Sweaty palms
- Check
- Sore throat
- / Check
- / And all of this is in books
- Written down
- All of this is in lists
- To check off
- In statistics
- Pie graphs
- To trade
- With other parents
- As you wave them / off
- As you wave them off to Grade Two camp
- But?
- But there are some things that aren't
- In the books
- That aren't written down
- Like
- Swine flu
- And then you have to guess
- Guess or google it
- I guess, but
- Don't you think that is scary?
- That there are these
- Diseases
- These illnesses
- Online
- Out there
- That you don't know about
- Don't you think that is fucking terrifying?
- That some bug is just waiting under the skin of some
- Of some Mexican farm worker until / they
- *Bam!*

- Travel across the world and infect your child and you don't even know what you're supposed to do
- It's not in the book!
- You don't even know what the illness is, or that she even has anything at all
- You don't even know what it means until
- Until your husband calls you and tells you that your teenage daughter has to die
- For the good of mankind
- And that you have to tell her
- May I add
- Grown child
- Fifteen years old
- Fourteen years old
- Dead
- For the good of mankind
- And you take her into your bedroom
- I'll take care of this
- Mother's work
- And I put her on the bed
- Our bed
- Because walking her upstairs
- To her bed
- With this knowledge
- Seems a bit much
- A tad bit much
- In this state
- So you put her on the bed
- Our bed
- 'What's wrong?'
- But the mother doesn't answer
- The daughter has a pimple on the left side of her chin
- Red and young
- Pushing out the skin
- 'What's wrong?'
- They'd only just started popping up
- And the bathroom

- Full of creams
- And wipes
- That she religiously applied
- As if it was her fault
- That they popped
- 'It's not your fault'
- 'What?'
- 'Nothing'
- Daughter looks worried now
- 'Is it about Dad?"
- Having a father in the army is a funny thing
- One foot out
- One foot in
- Always waiting for the phone call
- Never ready for it when it comes
- 'No'
- Mother lies
- It is about Dad
- It's about Dad and his fucking army
- His fucking pride
- 'Mum, you're freaking me out'
- His stupid brother
- 'Mum!'
- Mum is vomiting now
- On the bed
- The comforter
- Our comforter
- 'Mum'
- 'Do you have cancer?'
- 'Is Dad leaving?'
- 'Is E sick?'
- Mother doesn't know what to say
- Even if
- Through the vomiting
- The hiccups
- Sick warm on her lap
- How do you tell your daughter what your husband has told you

- She will die tomorrow
- Because there is no guide book
- That tells you what to do
- What to say
- To your daughter
- Just getting pimples
- Who your husband
- Has sentenced to death
- For everyone else's children
- Who looks you in the face and asks you
- 'Mum, what's wrong?'
- Mother is vomiting
- There is no checklist
- So keep that in mind

19. BEFORE IT ALL

- Before
- Before it all
- We
- You
- We were a family
- One
- Two
- Three
- Four
- Five
- And sitting
- Six
- And sitting
- Yes, look at us all sit
- Back for a meal
- Fadduh home
- Happy
- Happy cos work went well
- And he was back
- Back for a meal
- And

- We ate
- Drank
- Smiled
- Laughed
- The smart one got her pen license
- A year early too
- Everyone at their correct spot
- Muddah
- Fadduh
- Sister
- Brudda
- Sister
- Everyone at their correct / spot
- Sister?
- Fadduh?
- Sister?
- Fadduh?

20. SATURN RETURNS II

ORESTES *has come to visit* ELECTRA *again. He has brought her McDonald's, which she gorges on as they talk.*

ORESTES: I sent you a message.
ELECTRA: I didn't get it.
ORESTES: It doesn't matter.
ELECTRA: Are you drunk?
ORESTES: No.
ELECTRA: It doesn't matter. Let's go through it again.
ORESTES: It is through.
ELECTRA: Again.
ORESTES: We have done this—
ELECTRA: Please.
ORESTES: Saturday morning.
ELECTRA: At ten thirty.
ORESTES: Saturday morning, at ten thirty.
ELECTRA: Ish.
ORESTES: He will arrive home.

ELECTRA: Through which door?

ORESTES: The back door.

ELECTRA: Yes. He will use the back door so he can drop his swimming gear in the laundry.

ORESTES: And I will be waiting.

ELECTRA: She will be at spinning class.

ORESTES: Spinning class ends at eleven o'clock. She comes home and repeat.

ELECTRA: And what?

ORESTES: And she comes home and I fucking cook her breakfast, what do you think?

ELECTRA: Do you realise they have a special dinner, on the day that Dad died. Every year, a special dinner. She can't remember my fucking birthday but, no fail, they remember this.

ORESTES: I get it.

ELECTRA: Do you? I have been waiting for you, waiting for you for years to come back.

ORESTES: But why? If you've got it so sorted out, why haven't you just done it yourself?

ELECTRA: I would really appreciate it if you didn't come to visit me drunk.

ORESTES:

ELECTRA:

ORESTES: Saturday, at ten thirty-ish, I will be waiting.

ELECTRA: Blood for blood.

21. HAPPY FAMILIES

- And we didn't see Mum for a while
- Me and
- My sister, just the two
- We were shuffled around
- Family friend to family
- Friend
- We ate McDonald's
- For dinner
- And didn't have to go to school
- For ages

- And ages
- We watched tellie
- Painted our nails
- And we played ads
- And one day
- One day while playing
- Coles New World!
- Ads
- She came in
- Which in retrospect
- In retrospect it was kind of weird cos
- 'You killed Dad!'
- And
- That's just not
- She came in and told you that you and your sister had to go
- Go with her
- 'What?'
- 'Your aunty's not in, is she?'
- 'You killed Dad!'
- And your sister jumps up
- 'Mummmmm!'
- Your sister jumps up
- Traitorous with glee
- Away from you
- Away from the game
- Traitorous
- 'Mummm!'
- But not you
- Not you
- You can see him
- Outside
- Smoking a cigarette on the lawn
- On the lawn outside
- Looking towards the front door
- Waiting
- 'Come on, E'
- She's talking to you now

- 'No'
- 'Come on, E'
- She's talking to you, and you
- You turn away and you concentrate on the TV screen
- On the ads
- Cos you really really really like this game
- And you need to think of something-not-this
- Cos this is not—
- 'Come on, Electra'
- *'No!'*
- But she
- The there-but-not
- The mother
- She grabs your arm
- One of you starts to cry
- Not you
- The other one
- Starts to cry
- But it doesn't matter
- Your arm is pulling but you won't get up
- You don't stop watching the ads
- Red Rooster!
- She pulls you by your arm across the floor
- The carpet burning
- Commonwealth Bank!
- But it doesn't matter
- Nothing matters
- You will never
- Ever
- Call her Mother

22. EMPATHY GROUP

ELECTRA *says her goodbyes at the hospital.*

ELECTRA: I'd like to thank all of you.
   When I was young I saw a man bleed to death.
   We were told not to look.

A woman, a policewoman we didn't know, picked us up.
We couldn't walk.
We had been lying there for forty-eight hours.
He had been lying there for forty-eight hours.
The woman asked us if we were okay.
My sister vomited on her.
We had both shat on ourselves.
There was piss in our hair.
When the policemen carried us downstairs they said:
Don't look to your left, keep looking at me, keep looking at—
But I looked left.
She didn't.
She kept looking at her policeman.
I looked left.
He was under a sheet. I could see his
And the twisted
His brown stains across the tiles
Trying to get out
Trying to get help
We were upstairs
For forty-eight hours
I am going home now.

23. *DEATH OF THE MUDDAH*

Just the head of ELECTRA. *During the killing of her mother. We hear the initial blow, she doesn't flinch. With every utterance of 'Again' blood splatters on her face until her face is red with blood.*

ELECTRA: Again. Again. Again. Again. Again. Again.

24. *PLAIN AS A PICTURE TAKE TWO*

- There was this guy
- No, man
- No
- Sorry
- There was this prince
- I went to school with him

- He was a year above me
- No, below me
- A year above me
- And
- And he had three sisters
- So, sorry, there was three girls /
- Princesses and
- And him. Baby boy
- The princesses were famous at their school
- House captains and
- Did stuff like spoke at assembly
- Raised money for disabled people and horses
- And they were hot
- Pretty
- Smoking
- And they were the star of many scribbles on the back of toilet doors
- But he didn't go to their school
- Thank God
- So he didn't know
- About the scribbles
- Thank God
- But he went to our school
- And he made his own splash
- His own indent on the back of toilet walls
- When he went back home for Easter break
- One year
- And
- Murdered his mum
- And her husband
- Apparently
- Apparently he had been planning it for years
- While we were sitting next to him in class
- While we were working on that Maths project
- The Australian boy with the endless money
- And absent family
- Went home and didn't play nice

- You would have never guessed it
- At first
- At school
- At first at school they had tried to not tell us
- To keep it secret
- To keep it contained
- But it wasn't long before everyone knew
- And found the blog
- Of course
- The papers called it:
- 'The nutty writings of an angry teenage boy'
- As if that was a thing
- And some of us
- Breathed a sigh of relief
- Cos it could have easily been us
- Murdered by this psycho
- Machine gun to rollcall
- Who can kill their own mother?
- You would never have guessed it
- Our parents were called
- The blog had our school in the header
- Moron
- So we all had to be therapised
- And people in the street looked at us funny
- Girl schools recanted social mixers
- As if
- As if being a psycho is contagious
- Thanks asshole
- And then the trial happened
- Closed because of his age
- Open because of the internet
- And stories of his mother's indiscretions came out
- Of sleeping with his father's murderer
- Of celebrating his death day with crazy kinky sex parties
- Well that's what the blogs said
- And closed case
- We only had the blogs to go by

- And outside the courthouse
- He walked tall
- Taller than he ever looked here
- And newspaper stories from Australia called him
- Striking
- Handsome
- And not that I'm gay or anything
- But he was
- He totally was hot
- Hotter than he ever looked here
- And people
- Online and
- Not
- Online
- People everywhere were coming to his defence
- A boy protecting his family
- His father
- His name

From left: Kate Cheel as Electra, Liam Nunan as Orestes and Contessa Treffone as Chrysothemis in Griffin Independent's 2015 production of MinusOneSister *in Sydney. (Photo: Brett Boardman)*

- A lion
- A king
- A lion king
- People everywhere were speaking up for the guy from Eleven-B that didn't speak all that much
- Who didn't have a date to the winter social
- Whose name did not ring any bells
- Because he was right
- He had done something wrong to right a wrong and he was right
- Right
- And he was finally where he belonged
- In his kingdom
- And it became so obvious to us that we never really knew him
- That time we played soccer after badminton practice
- Or the school play rehearsals where he rigged the lights
- He wasn't really there
- He was busy
- Plotting his return
- He was in juvy for only a couple of months
- He was released a hero
- I never saw him in the flesh again
- I went to school with him
- He was a year above me
- No, below me
- A year above me

25. ANOTHER DAY, ANOTHER FUNERAL

ELECTRA *and* CHRYSOTHEMIS *outside their mother's funeral.*

CHRYSOTHEMIS: Black, once again.
ELECTRA: It was right.
CHRYSOTHEMIS: Don't you ever get sick of black?
ELECTRA: She ruined our family.
CHRYSOTHEMIS: When do you think she wrote it?
ELECTRA: What?
CHRYSOTHEMIS: The will.

ELECTRA: I don't know. I think even he was surprised with the reading.
CHRYSOTHEMIS: His lawyer told him?
ELECTRA: Yes. He said he would split it.
CHRYSOTHEMIS: Bullshit.
ELECTRA: Well he said we could have some shares, we could live in the house.
CHRYSOTHEMIS: How very kind.
ELECTRA: It is his house.
CHRYSOTHEMIS: His house that he has not stepped foot in since he was six years old.
ELECTRA: Yes.
CHRYSOTHEMIS: What have you done?
ELECTRA: It was our right.
CHRYSOTHEMIS: Your right? Revenge is inheritance, inheritance that is not ours to claim.
ELECTRA:
CHRYSOTHEMIS: We are all that's left.
ELECTRA: I know.
CHRYSOTHEMIS: There is nothing left.
ELECTRA: I know.
CHRYSOTHEMIS: Do you feel better now?
ELECTRA: I don't know.
CHRYSOTHEMIS: Everyone at their correct spot.

26. THE TRICK TO ADS

- There is a trick
- A talent that seems
- Natural
- But is learnt
- From sister to sister
- It is taught through
- Competition
- Jealousy
- Tension
- You know how girls get
- A keen eye

- A strong drive for context
- For detail and
- Context
- So that within the first second
- Yes, even the first half-second
- You can tell what the ad is
- It seems impossible at first
- How could she get Latina Fresh from half a second
- But look
- Look
- If you notice the telltale signs of Italian family
- *La familia*
- The red checked cloth on the dinner table
- The grains in the ja/r
- Latina Fresh!
- And that's how it goes
- The girls
- The sisters
- The three sisters
- They learnt this game well
- Well like anyone would have a talent
- Like arithmetic, or spelling
- Like cobbling or the MS read-a-thon
- They learnt it well
- A middle-aged woman on screen by herself
- Omo!
- Sunny day
- Metamucil!
- Grey day at work
- Reflex paper!
- Fadduh
- Muddah
- At a table
- Fadduh
- Cooking
- Muddah rolling her eyes
- The kids in on this

- The muddah and the kids
- Rolling their eyes
- The fadduh proud
- Proud as punch
- As punch
- That he'd made a meal
- He made a meal
- And they can all forget
- All forget all the crappy things that happened that day
- The teasing
- The assessments
- The cyberbullying
- The sexting
- The texting
- The 'Glee'
- They all forget and they're happy
- Fadduh is home
- Back for a meal
- Happy
- Happy cos work went well
- And he was back
- Back for a meal
- We
- You
- We were a family
- One
- Two
- Three
- Four
- Five
- Six
- And sitting
- Yes, look at us all sit
- And
- We ate
- Drank
- Smiled

- Laughed
- Everyone at their correct spot
- Muddah
- Fadduh
- Sister
- Brudda
- Sister
- Sister
- Everyone at their correct spot

THE END

Sarah Ward as Bobby in NEON Festival of Independent Theatre's 2015 production of SHIT in Melbourne. (Photo: Sebastian Bourges)

SHIT
Patricia Cornelius

Patricia Cornelius is a playwright, screenwriter and novelist. Her most recent play, *SHIT*, was presented at the 2017 Sydney Festival, following its 2015 Melbourne premiere as part of MTC's NEON Season and its 2016 remount at 45Downstairs. Her play, *Savages* (45Downstairs), won the Victorian Premier's Literary Award for Drama in 2014 and the Green Room Award for Writing and was nominated for an AWGIE and the Griffin Prize. Over her career Patricia has written over 25 plays which include *Big Heart*, *Do Not Go Gentle*, *The Call*, *Love*, *Fever*, *Boy Overboard*, *Slut* and *Who's Afraid of the Working Class?* (co-written with Andrew Bovell, Christos Tsiolkas, Melissa Reeves and Irine Vela).

Other playwriting awards include Victorian and NSW Premiers' Literary Awards (2011), Patrick White Playwright's Award, Richard Wherrett Prize, Wal Cherry Award and nine AWGIES for stage, community theatre, and theatre for young people. She won the Australian Writers' Foundation Playwriting Award (2015), a Patrick White Fellowship (2012), a Fellowship from the Australia Council's Theatre Board, as well as the AWGIE Major Award three times. She is a founding member of Melbourne Workers' Theatre.

Patricia co-wrote the feature film adaptation, *Blessed*, based on the play *Who's Afraid of the Working Class?* (for which she won an AWGIE), and she is currently developing a feature film. Her novel, *My Sister Jill*, was published by Random House. Many of her plays are published by Currency Press.

SHIT was first produced by Dee & Cornelius at the NEON Festival of Independent Theatre, Melbourne, on 25 June 2015, with the following cast:

SAM	Peta Brady
BOBBY	Sarah Ward
BILLY	Nicci Wilks

Director, Susie Dee
Set and Costume Designer, Marg Horwell
Lighting Designer, Rachel Burke
Sound Designer, Anna Liebzeit
Production and Stage Manager, Bec Moore
Producer, Ebony Bott

CHARACTERS

BOBBY

SAM

BILLY

There's not a single moment when the three young women transcend their ugliness. There's no indication of a better or in fact any inner life. They don't believe in anything. They're mean, downmouthed, downtrodden, hard bit, utterly damaged women. They're neither salt of the earth nor sexy. They love no-one and no-one loves them. They believe the world is shit, that their lives are shit, that they are shit.

SETTING

There are two intertwined narratives.
One is played out in a room.
The other is played out in a series of images, at another time, in another place.

A slash (/) indicates a point of interruption in a line of dialogue.

Prologue. Lights up on BILLY.

BILLY: And he goes, look at you, fuck look at you, what the fuck you done, you fucking done nothing, you never fucking going do something, you fucked-up waste of space, what fucking contribution you made, nothing, nothing at all, you fucked-up nothing, fucking nothing you are, a big fucking nothing, he goes, the biggest fucking nothing, the biggest fucking nothing I know, and I think, who's this fucking fucked-up fuck telling me I'm fucked up, who's he, and I go, who are you to fucking tell me I'm fucking nothing, you fucking fuck, you're the fucking nothing, never going to fucking do nothing fuck, what contribution you and you're fucking telling me I'm fucking nothing makes you fucking way more fucking way more, way way more fucking nothing.

    Silence.

What?

    BOBBY *and* SAM *step in. They stare at* BILLY.

BOBBY: Listen to you!
BILLY: What?
SAM: Fucking over the top.
BILLY: So?
BOBBY: How many fucks you stuffed in that sentence?
BILLY: So?
SAM: Too many fucks.
BOBBY: You sound fucking nuts with the fucking fucking stuff.
SAM: Way over.
BILLY: Too bad, I like it.
BOBBY: I like it just don't lay it on so fucking thick.
SAM: Thick carpet of fucks.
BOBBY: Way too thick.
BILLY: I don't give a shit.
BOBBY: I don't give a shit either but you're not …
BILLY: What?
BOBBY: You're not …

BILLY: What, fuck you, what?
BOBBY: Using it well.
BILLY: Using it well?
SAM: That's it, you're not.
BILLY: Fuck me. I know how to use it. Go to hell.
BOBBY: You're not making the best of it.
BILLY: I know how to make the best of it.
BOBBY: You wear it out.
BILLY: I'll wear it any fucking way I want to.
SAM: You do, you wear it thin.
BILLY: Here we go, this time the fucking carpet's thin.
SAM: She can't stop it.
BILLY: I can fucking stop it.
BOBBY: I know she can't.
BILLY: I can fucking stop.
SAM: She's chronic.
BOBBY: Probably the first word she ever said.
BILLY: Fuck off!
SAM: Cute.
BOBBY: Sort of.
SAM: I like little kids who swear.
BOBBY: She's grown up with it.
SAM: I guess.
BOBBY: Doesn't know any better.
SAM: Yes. For her it's like saying please.
BILLY: It is, fuck you.
BOBBY: Cunt comes later.
SAM: Not that much later.
BOBBY: When you're a bit older, cunt comes.
SAM: What? Like three?
BILLY: They're the best.
BOBBY/SAM: They are.
BILLY: I like them. I like them so much.
SAM: They're like …
BILLY: Like bullets.
BOBBY: From a shotgun.
SAM: A machine gun.

BOBBY: An AK.
BILLY: Like the sharpest blade.
BOBBY: A razor blade.
SAM: A machete.
BILLY: A switch.
SAM: They're the strongest.
BOBBY: By far.
SAM: Fuck and …
ALL: Cunt.
SAM: Can't get no better.
BOBBY: But no good if they're overdone.
BILLY: Alright! What do you want?
BOBBY: Just tone it down, would you?
BILLY: What do you think I am? A nun?
SAM: Don't overdo it.
BILLY: I'm addicted.
SAM: So am I.
BILLY: Couldn't give them up if I tried.
SAM: No way.
BILLY: And who wants to try?
BOBBY: They're strong.
BILLY: Powerful.
SAM: Fucking powerful.
BILLY: Tough words.
SAM: Fucking tough.
BOBBY: Frightening.
SAM: For some.
BOBBY: For most.
BILLY: You say fuck or cunt, you watch them run.
BOBBY: I've seen it with my own two eyes. On the train or the tram or the bus, I seen someone talking the talk, fuck this, fuck that, fuck him, fuck that cunt, that fucking cunt, you fucking cunt. You got it? With me? They've got their heads buried, they've got the sweat pouring, dripping off their foreheads, they're squirming, they're shitting themselves, they're running for the doors, they're dinging the bells, they're yelling, next stop, next stop please.
SAM: I know, I know, I've seen that. I've done that.

BOBBY: I've made them run like that.
BILLY: Who hasn't?
SAM: It's fucking funny.
BILLY: Watch them cunts go running.
BOBBY: The life in them words.
BILLY: Electrifying.
SAM: It's sort of surprising.
BILLY: Them words been around for years.
BOBBY: They hurt them, them words hurt them.
BILLY: They burn them.
SAM: They sting them.
BOBBY: They make them bleed.
SAM: I've had them women go, watch your language please.
BOBBY: I've had them.
BILLY: Plenty of them fucking bitches.
BOBBY: I say, what you going do? Ring the police?
SAM: I hate them bitches.
BILLY: I hate them too.
SAM: Looking down their noses.
BILLY: They're words, bitches.
BOBBY: Words.
SAM: Just words.
BILLY: Fucking words.
BOBBY: What's wrong with the cunts?
BILLY: I have no fucking idea.
SAM: It's not ladylike.
BOBBY: Ladylike.
SAM: It's not.
BOBBY: Of course it's fucking not.
BILLY: They don't like girls talking it.
BOBBY: Who tell it.
BILLY: Like it fucking is.
BOBBY: They like us quiet.
SAM: Like mice.
BOBBY: They like us soft.
SAM: Like kittens.
BILLY: Ladylike.

BOBBY: Ladylike. They like us to listen.
BILLY: To their every word.
BOBBY: Not talk.
BILLY: Say nothing.
BOBBY: Just listen, and nod our heads.
They nod.
BILLY: Fuck that for a joke.
BOBBY: They think we're foul-mouthed sluts.
SAM: We are.
BILLY: I'm not a slut, you slut.
SAM: Don't call me a slut.
BOBBY: Shut up, you're both sluts.
BILLY: They think we're dumb.
SAM: I'm not dumb.
BILLY: They think you are.
BOBBY: They think we can't string a fucking sentence together without swearing.
BILLY: I can't.
BOBBY: You can.
SAM: I'm not sure she can.
BILLY: Can you?
BOBBY: 'Course I can.
BILLY: Try it.
SAM: Say something.
BOBBY: Alright.
SAM: Without one fuck or cunt.
BILLY: Or any other fucking swearing.
BOBBY: Alright.
SAM: Come on.
BOBBY: Okay, okay, hang on.
BILLY: Say something.
BOBBY: Hello, my name is Bobby and I couldn't give a fuck … Oh fuck!
They hoot with laughter.
SAM: I've got it. Hello. I'm … Sam. I've … lived … in … nearly … every … suburb … in this … city …
BOBBY: You … sound … like … a fucking idiot.

BILLY: Alright, shut up. Here I go. Hiya, I'm Billy and I'm not afraid of anyone. I've never been afraid of anyone, no cop, no teacher, no man, not a single person have I ever been afraid of.
SAM: You did it!
BILLY: Of course I fucking did. I can fucking talk like them cunts.
The others point accusingly at her swearing.
I meant to do that.
SAM: You fucking did not.
BILLY: I did!
BOBBY: I don't care what they think of us. I don't care if they think I'm dumb, a slut, a fucking dog. I know I'm not them. I don't want to be them.
BILLY: Got a problem with how we talk …
ALL: Fuck off.
BILLY: Don't like what we have to say …
ALL: Fuck off.
BILLY: Don't want to listen to our story …
They indicate: 'Fuck off'.
BOBBY: Their life's shit, our life's shit, just different shit.
BILLY: Yeah.
SAM: That's right.

They click their fingers. The three women walk in sync, as one. They stop, they click their fingers and the sound reverberates: a small homage to West Side Story. *They walk on. One leads with a different move, then another leads, and again. This gang of three are smooth and well-practised in the routine.*

A room.

BILLY: Sandra says I seen you looking at him and I said I didn't fucking look at him, why would I fucking look at him, I've got no reason to fucking look at him.
SAM/BOBBY: You were looking at him.
BILLY: I wasn't looking at him. I was looking like I was looking at you or anybody else who spoke. I wasn't *looking* at him. I wasn't fucking looking looking. I was just looking when he said something like

when you're at the shop and somebody says, can I help you, and you fucking look at them because they're fucking talking to you and you say, yes, give us some smokes. That's how I was looking at him and if that cunt thinks I was looking at him any other way then she can fucking get fucked.
BOBBY: Sandra is fucked.
SAM: Totally.
BILLY: I wasn't fucking looking at him.

Silence.

SAM: What are we going to tell them?

Pause.

BILLY/BOBBY: Nothing.

The sound of footsteps. High-heel ones.
The three women appear in silhouette. They are completely still, hunched slightly, poised, listening intensely.

From left: Peta Brady as Sam, Nicci Wilks as Billy and Sarah Ward as Bobby in NEON Festival of Independent Theatre's 2015 production of SHIT in Melbourne. (Photo: Sebastian Bourges)

A room.

SAM: Do you think anything could save us?

    Pause.

BILLY: No.

BOBBY: Like God, do you mean?

    Pause.

BILLY: No.

BOBBY: Like someone puts their hand in and pulls you out before you drown?

BILLY: Like someone says, you're right, you're right, I got you.

BOBBY: Like someone shoots a crocodile just before it gets you.

BILLY: Like a doctor cuts out the rot before it infects you.

BOBBY: Like when you jump someone's going to catch you.

BILLY: Like someone puts their mouth on yours and blows air in you.

BOBBY: Like someone says, keep away from her or I'll kill you.

BILLY: Like when a boulder comes pounding down and Superman scoops you up in his arms.

BOBBY: Like someone grabs you just before …

SAM: Alright, alright.

BILLY: Sam, nothing's going to save us.

BOBBY: Too late to save us.

BILLY: Way too fucking late.

BOBBY: We're past saving.

BILLY: Way past saving.

SAM: Maybe someone could've saved us when we were little.

BILLY: Doubt it.

SAM: When we were three.

BOBBY: From the moment I came out nothing could save me.

BILLY: From the moment my mum got knocked up nothing could save me.

SAM: Nothing at all?

    Pause.

BILLY: A bedroom with a lock on the door.

    They laugh.

There are ones who listen to music all the time.
SAM: I did that.
BOBBY: Well?
SAM: It cut down the shouting.
BILLY: In one of the houses I was in a girl read books.
SAM: Did that save her?
BILLY: Sort of. For a while. I saw her off her fucking face when she was about twelve.
BOBBY: Drugs can save you.
BILLY/SAM: Drugs can save you.
SAM: When they're in good supply.
BILLY: I used to think someone was going to save me.
SAM: Me too.
BILLY: Pick me up and carry me off ... somewhere.
SAM: Me too.
BILLY: And tell me good things.
SAM: Like, you're a good girl.
BILLY: Well done, you did real good,
BOB: You sat up straight.
BILLY: You didn't pick your face.
SAM: You ate, good girl, you ate.
BOBBY: You laughed in the right place.
SAM: You're pretty when you smile.
BILLY: You enjoyed yourself, didn't you?
SAM: You thought about someone else for a change.
BOBBY: You didn't spit in anyone's face.
BILLY: Like someone who gives a shit, who says, I'm here for you, you know that, don't you?
BOBBY: And says, do you understand, are you listening to me?
SAM: Look at me.
BILLY: Look at my face.
ALL: You're ... worth ... something.

Pause.

SAM: What's her name?
BILLY: What?
SAM: Got to give her a name, this woman who could've saved us.
BILLY: What?!

BOBBY: Caitlin. How about that?
SAM: Caitlin cuddles us.
BILLY: She bounces us on her knee.
BOBBY: I can't stand being fucking touched but I'll let Caitlin have a bit of a squeeze.
BILLY: Caitlin's got enormous tits and all she wants is to take us in her arms.
BOBBY: Oh, yes please.
SAM: To make us happy.
BOBBY: To smooth away the pain.
SAM: To love us.
BOBBY: To stop Billy from saying fuck.
BILLY: And from Bobby calling her a cunt.
SAM: And from biting her neck and draining her blood.
BILLY: Caitlin might have saved us.
BOBBY: I had a Caitlin. For about a year I had her. When I was about eight, maybe nine, I know I wasn't with her when I was ten. She had these huge tits and she'd grab me and tuck me into them. I'd be standing there and she'd grab me. I'd be on the couch watching TV and she'd grab me. On my way to bed, to school, just have to move and she'd grab me and squeeze the fucking shit out of me. Squeeze me every chance she'd get. Squeeze the life out of me. Squeeze me to death. I used to have to hold my breath. Then when I was ten someone else had me.
SAM: Couldn't she save you?
BOBBY: No, too far gone.
SAM: What she doing squeezing you all the time?
BOBBY: Loved me, I guess.
SAM: Fuck me!
BILLY: I never had one of them Caitlins.
SAM: Neither did I. I love her. I love Caitlin.
BILLY: I had cold fucking fish bitches.
SAM: The sit up straight, don't touch that, that's enough, you greedy guts kind.
BILLY: The stop that, and stop that, don't do that kind.
BOBBY: One I had treated her dogs better than me.
BILLY: I had one I liked. She was nice.

BOBBY: They'd growl at me when I had to get up and have a wee.
BILLY: Then I got sent back to Mum.
SAM: That happened to me sometimes.
BOBBY: Most of the time I'd piss my bed.
BILLY: Never had one of them big-titty cuddly ones.
BOBBY: Whenever I could I'd kick the shit out of them dogs.
SAM: Fuck, Bobby, it's not the dogs' fucking fault.
BILLY: Men, I had them.
SAM: Plenty of them.
BILLY: Too many.
SAM: The sit on my knee and give us a kiss kind.
BILLY: The tongue slipping between your lips kind.
SAM: This is just between you and me kind.
BILLY: This is our secret kind.
SAM: The stink of their breath.
BILLY: Fuck! I can feel their whiskers.
SAM: And their fat fingers.
BILLY: And their hard dicks.
BOBBY: Yeah well, boohoo, never mind.

In marvellous synchronisation they parody the sadness of their situation, heads bowed low, backs bent, grotesque gestures, their faces pulled in exaggerated misery.

A room.

BILLY: Some bitch in the house was talking and she says, there's nothing can be done, she's too far gone. Forsaken, she said. Forsaken. I think, what's this forsaken? Forsaken like something taken like from the Bible. Something totally fucked. And then I know who she's talking about, who's this forsaken, who's too far gone, past saving. I start laughing. It's this Danni chick who's a fat ugly bitch and I think she is, she's forfuckingsaken, no doubt about it, spot on, got it in one. She hasn't got a chance in hell. And then the bitch keeps on talking, and it's me she's talking about, I'm the one who's fucked, who's forsaken. It's me. I'm forsaken! Me! Fuck. Fuck off. Me? Fucking forsaken. Me?!

A room.

SAM: Sandra.
BOBBY: Fuck, man, fuck!
SAM: Her face.
BOBBY: Smashed.
SAM: Her nose be broke.
BOBBY: For sure.
SAM: Her eye socket too.
BOBBY: I reckon.
SAM: Other bones too.
BOBBY: Ribs …
SAM: Yeah.
BOBBY: Collarbone …
SAM: Likely.
BOBBY: And stuff inside where he put the boot in.
SAM: Spleen maybe.
BOBBY: Or kidney.
SAM: She'll have a bald spot where he pulled her hair out.
BILLY: I've had that, it'll grow back.

    BOBBY *touches her head.*

BOBBY: I don't know about that.
SAM: I could see it coming.
BOBBY: Craig was just waiting for the opportunity.
SAM: And she gave it to him.
BOBBY: Shut the fuck up, Sandra, shut up.
SAM: She never shuts up.
BOBBY: Go fucking quiet, you stupid bitch, bite your tongue.
BILLY: Stupid she is.
SAM: Fucking is.
BOBBY: Can't she see that Craig's arcing up.
SAM: Gone dead in the eyes.
BOBBY: Gone too quiet.
SAM: Looking at her like … with that smile.
BOBBY: Is she fucking blind?
SAM: Blah di blah blah blah, on and on. 'You're a fucking bastard, Craig, I saw you looking at that bitch, you're nothing but a fucking shit.'

BOBBY: Oh my God, you brainless bitch.
SAM: Dumb as dog shit.
BILLY: Stupid cunt.
BOBBY: And in Craig goes.
SAM: No holding back.
BOBBY: Brutal.
SAM: Brutal.
BOBBY: She'll go back.
SAM: She won't.
BOBBY: You watch her.
SAM: She won't.
BOBBY: I'll give her a month.
BILLY: Stupid cunt.
BOBBY: Some girls bring it on.
BILLY: I'd punch her too the way she goes on.
BOBBY/SAM: Brutal.
BILLY: I love a good fight.
BOBBY: That was not a fight.
SAM: Shit no, not a fair one.
BOBBY: That was a massacre.
BILLY: Alright. I mean a real one, when you see stars, when you taste blood where your teeth have bitten into your lip. I love them. Even when I lose them. They're like I'm the king of the world. Come on! Take me on! Try it! Love it. Come on, Bobby, how about a round?
BOBBY: No thanks.
BILLY: We'll stop when we draw blood.
BOBBY: No.
BILLY: You scared?
BOBBY: Terrified.
BILLY: Think you are. Think the old Bobby has lost her nerve.
BOBBY: You're right, I've lost it.
BILLY: Don't be a fucking pussy. Fight me.
BOBBY: Call me a pussy, I don't care.
BILLY: Come on.
SAM: Didn't you hear her?
BILLY: What's it got to do with you?
BOBBY: She's my protector. She'll fight you instead.

SAM: I've never seen you back down from a fight.

BOBBY: I don't want to fight Billy. I've fought her. I don't need to fight her again.

SAM: I've never seen you lose.

BOBBY: I've lost plenty. Too many. It took me a long time to learn when to fight and when to go doormat. You fight someone who will not hesitate to smash you fair square in the face or throat or guts, you just fucked yourself. If he's pissed or out of it and you're sure he won't remember, then fucking fight, hit him hard in the nuts, bash his head with a brick, knock him out. But if he's with it, go soft, drop like a cake, all your weight, go limp and cover your face and hope to fucking God he won't lift you and hit you or while you're down kick you.

BILLY: It's a risk playing dead.

BOBBY: It is.

BILLY: Because he could lay into you.

BOBBY: You hope he'll forget you're there.

SAM: That's when some of them fuck you.

BOBBY: Yeah yeah.

From left: Nicci Wilks as Billy, Peta Brady as Sam and Sarah Ward as Bobby in NEON Festival of Independent Theatre's 2015 production of SHIT in Melbourne. (Photo: Sebastian Bourges)

SAM: They do.
BILLY: Let's not go there.
BOBBY: It takes ages to get over a beating. It wrecks your face. It breaks bones. It kills, a beating does, it fucking kills.

Pause.

SAM: Like Sandra.
BOBBY: Like Sandra.
SAM: Sandra be crying.
BOBBY: For a long time.

BOBBY, BILLY *and* SAM *dance in an aggressive frenzy. The dance bleeds quickly into frenzied kicks and punches thrown at some imagined victim. Occasionally they come together and dance as one.*

A room.

SAM: I'm with this family. They've got kids, two girls older than me, and a boy.
BOBBY: A boy.
SAM: A little boy. Pretty.
BILLY: A pretty boy.
SAM: About the same age as me. I'm four, I think, maybe more. I haven't been with them long. They're nice to me. I'm not hungry. We're at the beach and I've never been at the beach before and I don't like it much. The sand hurts between my toes and the water stings because my legs have got sores on them. I'm watching the boy, the pretty boy. They tell me he's my brother and them girls are my sisters but they're not.
BILLY: I hate that.
BOBBY: I don't like that sort of shit.
BILLY: All of a sudden we're a family.
BOBBY: As if.
SAM: He's full of himself, so full, full to overflowing with himself. They love him. They love him this family. His sisters do anything he wants and he wants a lot. He orders them about. He stands with his hands on his hips and shouts. Sometimes he smacks them and leaves a red mark on their skin and then he cries because he's sorry he's hurt them.

They kiss him and kiss him and his head falls back and he giggles, the pretty boy, beautiful really, laughs and laughs. His father picks him up. He's told me he's my father too.
BILLY: More of that shit.
BOBBY: Because he's not.
BILLY: Where do they get off?
SAM: He picks up the boy and swings him up on his shoulders and he stands at the water's edge. He points out to sea, the father does, as if he's saying to the boy, this is all yours for as far as you can see. The mother joins them, smiling up at them, her eyes for the boy, the boy, the boy is everything. Now his sisters are dancing around, adoring him. There's this terrible noise and it pierces their ears and it disturbs the peace this terrible noise and I can't believe it, it's come from me. A scream has come up like spew from deep inside of me. They look and when they see that the noise is mine, they laugh, and are drawn back to the beautiful boy, forgetting me. Later the boy is alone playing a game in the shallows. He's giving orders to the waves as if they're his men and he's leading them to shore. He's lost completely in his imagining, nothing to worry him, to distract him, to disturb him from this world he's in, a world I've never been in, never, not once, not even for a second. Suddenly a wave larger than the rest comes and topples him, and here's my chance.

Silence.

BILLY *and* BOBBY *step into the scene.*

BILLY/BOBBY: You got him?

SAM *puts her hand out as if to hold down the boy's head.*

SAM: Yes, I got him.

BILLY *makes the same gesture.*

BILLY: I've got him.

BOBBY *makes the same gesture.*

BOBBY: I've got him.
BILLY: Is he struggling?
SAM: Not much.
BOBBY: Don't let him fool you.
SAM: When we going to let him up?

BILLY: We're not.
SAM: Got to let him up some time.
BOBBY: Why?
SAM: Not going to kill him, are we?
BILLY: Yep.
BOBBY: Why not?
SAM: Shit! I don't want to kill him.
BOBBY: Well, let him up.
SAM: I just wanted to frighten him a bit.
BILLY: Save him.
SAM: That's enough.
BOBBY: Better hurry up.
SAM: That's enough!

  BILLY *releases her hand.*

BILLY: Gone.

  BOBBY *releases her hand.*

BOBBY: Gone.

  SAM *releases her hand.*

SAM: Shit!
BOBBY: You stay with that family long?
SAM: Not long. They didn't like me.

  Pause. They laugh.

Sound of footsteps—high-heel ones. The women move fast. In and out of shadows, they dart. Finally they wait in ambush.

A room.

 When's the last time you cried?
BILLY: I never cried.
BOBBY: When you were a baby you would've cried.
BILLY: No.
BOBBY: All babies cry.
BILLY: Do they?
SAM: For a while they cry and then they stop.
BILLY: I don't remember crying. Even when I've been slapped or punched

or kicked, been square hit. Once I copped it right on the nose, my eyes watered and tears came down but they weren't tears, not real ones. I don't think I can.

SAM: You never been in that much pain?

BILLY: I don't feel pain.

BOBBY: Bullshit.

BILLY: I'm not making it up, I just don't feel it much. That's why I don't bother with slashing up. It does nothing for me. I get no release.

BOBBY: Bullshit. Come here and let's see if it's true. I'm happy to hurt you.

BILLY: I've got no time for tears. I hate cry babies, they shit me with their tears.

SAM: I don't cry.

BILLY: One boy I lived with cried all the time. You only had to look at him and he'd cry. He was the house punching bag. You'd pass him in the hallway and hit him, you'd sit and eat your dinner and kick him. He'd cry and someone would hit him to make him stop.

SAM: And did he?

BILLY: Of course not. I've faked it. Plenty of times I've turned it on.

She turns it on.

I'm sorry, I'm sorry, I didn't mean to. I won't do it again. I don't know why I did it. I'm so so so sorry.

And off.

Easy.

SAM: That's shit, listen to this,

She turns it on.

Don't hit me please, I'll do anything you want but please, don't, please don't, please don't hit me.

And off.

Should be on TV.

BILLY: Your turn.

BOBBY *turns it on. She's utterly convincing.*

BOBBY: Don't touch me, don't touch me. Don't. Don't. Please. Please. Please don't touch me.

And off.

How was I?

Pause.

BILLY: Fuck me, that was very good.
SAM: Should be on YouTube.
BOBBY: Thank you.
SAM: You telling me you never cried when you were a kid?
BILLY: Don't think I did.
SAM: What about crying because you feel sad or bad for someone?
BILLY: No.
BOBBY: What about at a sad film?
BILLY: No.
SAM: What about for yourself? Just cos you feel sad about … life or something else?
BILLY: No. Is that weird?
SAM: You never feel sad for anyone?
BILLY: No. Fuck them. Do you?
SAM: Yeah, sometimes. I think I do. I feel sad for my mum. Not so much now but when I was young I felt sad for her.
BILLY: I heard you.
SAM: What?
BILLY: I heard you crying for your mum.
SAM: Bull fucking shit, Billy, you did not!
BILLY: You were in the room next to mine and they came in and told you your mum wasn't coming and you cried your head off.
SAM: When was this?
BILLY: When we were in a resi unit one time.
SAM: That was a long time ago.
BOBBY: Where was I?
BILLY: You weren't in that one.
SAM: Now everything's fine with my mum. I see her all the time.
BILLY: When?
SAM: What?
BILLY: When do you see her?
SAM: I saw her not that long ago.
BILLY: How long?
BOBBY: Ease off, would you?

BILLY: Just interested that's all.
SAM: I don't know, a few weeks, months ago.
BILLY: Really?
SAM: You deaf or something? When's the last time you saw your mum?
BILLY: You kidding? I never see her. I fucking don't want to see her. I'd rather fucking die than see that cunt.
SAM: Oh my God, don't call your mum a cunt.
BILLY: I don't go for all this you've got to love your mum. I don't get it. My mum doesn't deserve to be loved. She's a cunt.
SAM: You shouldn't be angry with your mum.
BILLY: I'm not angry with her. I don't give a shit about her. I never think about her. Bobby's mum's a cunt too.
BOBBY: Don't call my mum a cunt.
BILLY: Sorry. But she is, isn't she?
BOBBY: Why bring my mum into this?
SAM: Yeah, fucking hell, Billy, leave her mum alone.
BOBBY: Oh fuck off, her mum's a fucking brain-dead junkie like mine.
BOBBY: Yeah, that might be the case but I love my mum.
BILLY: You do not!
SAM: Of course she does.
BILLY: No she doesn't.
SAM: Billy, she does.
BILLY: You don't. Do you?
BOBBY: No. She's a cunt.
SAM: Oh my God!
BOBBY: I used to cry when I got hurt. But not for a long time.
SAM: You don't cry because you feel sad?
BOBBY: I don't like it, crying, it's a waste of time.
SAM: You never feel sad?
BOBBY: No, not really.
SAM: Nor do I.
BILLY: I think it's all a lie, this feeling stuff. I don't reckon most people feel much. I think they feel fuck-all. I don't know anyone who is really kind. Do you?
BOBBY: There are kind people.
BILLY: Name one.
BOBBY: I don't know their names.

BILLY: Because they don't exist.
SAM: What about that Caitlin?
BILLY: She's weird, not kind.
BOBBY: There are kind people. Lots of them.
SAM: Like them who give money to the poor.
BOBBY: Exactly.
SAM: Or Africa.
BOBBY: Where people are dying from starvation.
SAM: I'm fucking starving.
BOBBY: So am I.
BILLY: Are they going to fucking feed us?
SAM: They have to, don't they?
BILLY: Are you going to feed us?!
BOBBY: They're not kind.
BILLY: They're taught not to be kind.
SAM: We're fucking starving in here!

They're on the hunt. Looking for someone. Anyone.

A room.

SAM: I want a horse. I want a dog, two dogs so they keep each other company. I want a house, a big one, and I want a pool and a barbeque and I want curtains on my bedroom window and a bed, queen-size, with sheets and doona. I want a fridge and I want it full of food, open it and stuff falls out it's so full—cheese, and marg and ice-cream, chocolate ice-cream. I want my life to be nice. I want good things in my life. I want …
BILLY: What right you got?
SAM: What?
BILLY: Just saying what right you got to want all this?
SAM: I can want.
BOBBY: Let her want shit.
BILLY: What makes you think you can want and want?
SAM: I can want, can't I?
BOBBY: She can want if she wants to.
BILLY: Who are you to want?
SAM: I'm just me. I'm like you or anybody else.

BILLY: No you're not.
SAM: I can want if you can want.
BILLY: I don't want. I don't want nothing.
SAM: I do, I want, I want things.
BILLY: Why do you?
SAM: What's fucking wrong with wanting things?
BILLY: It's pathetic.
BOBBY: It's a bit like you're still a kid.
SAM: Adults want things.
BOBBY: Like you're not full-grown.
BILLY: Like you're still on your mummy's tit.
SAM: Fuck off! I don't want like that!
BILLY: It's like you're not whole.
BOBBY: Like you got pieces missing.
BILLY: You're needy.
SAM: Wanting isn't needy. I'm not needy, I just want a few things.
BILLY: What? What is it exactly you want?
SAM: I want things. Stuff. Dogs and a fridge and stuff.
BILLY: You're wanting you're wanting you're wanting what?
SAM: I just said.
BOBBY: You want too much.
SAM: No, I don't.
BILLY: You're alright, aren't you?
SAM: Yeah, I'm alright, I'm alright.
BILLY: What's wrong with you?
SAM: Nothing.
BILLY: What's so bad about your life?
SAM: Nothing.
BILLY: What's with the wanting …
BOBBY: Something.
BILLY: Wanting …
BOBBY: This.
BILLY: Wanting …
BOBBY: That.
BILLY: Wanting …
BOBBY: Crap it sounds like to me.
SAM: What about a baby? Is there anything wrong with me wanting that?

BILLY: You want a baby?!
SAM: Yes, I think I do want one. It's natural to want a baby, you know.
BILLY: Natural?!
SAM: Most women want one.
BILLY: I don't want one.
SAM: I said most.
BILLY: What for?
SAM: What do you mean what for? Why do you think?
BILLY: For the cash you get.
SAM: No.
BILLY: Then why?
SAM: To love it, that's why.
BILLY: Fuck me, you want a baby so you can love it? What makes you think you're going to love it?
SAM: Because that's what happens when you have a baby. You love it.
BILLY: Did you love it?
BOBBY: Fuck off, Billy.
BILLY: Did you?
BOBBY: Shut the fuck up.
SAM: What are you talking about?
BILLY: Bobby had one and she didn't love it.
SAM: You had a baby?
BOBBY: Yes.
SAM: When?
BOBBY: Can't remember, years ago.
SAM: How old?
BOBBY: Twelve.
SAM: What happened to it?
BOBBY: Don't know.
SAM: What was it?
BOBBY: A baby.
SAM: A boy or a girl?
BOBBY: A boy or a girl.
SAM: Shit, you never told me you had a baby.
BOBBY: It was a long time ago.
SAM: You've never ever mentioned a baby.
BOBBY: I forgot.

BILLY: She had one and she didn't love it.
SAM: Didn't you?
BOBBY: No.
SAM: Do you think about it?
BOBBY: No.
SAM: Do you want to see it?
BOBBY: No.
SAM: Do you think you'll ever …
BOBBY: No no no no no.
BILLY: You want a baby.
SAM: It'd love me.
BILLY: You're a baby. You're a big fucking baby.
SAM: Why you being so mean to me?
BILLY: I'm not being mean to you.
BOBBY: Are a bit.
BILLY: No, I'm not.
BOBBY: A bit mean.
SAM: A lot fucking mean.
BILLY: I'm trying to help her out.
BOBBY: Doesn't sound like that to me.
BILLY: Don't want her to be disappointed.
SAM: Forget it, forgive me for thinking I might like to change something?
BILLY: Now we're getting somewhere. Is that it? You want to change something?
SAM: I wouldn't mind a change.
BILLY: Want your face lifted, want your tits big, want duck lips?
SAM: Fucking hell, forget it, I don't want nothing. I don't want to change nothing, I don't want, from now, I got no wants.
BILLY: Just asking.
SAM: I don't want to talk to you anymore, you fuck with my head.

A room.

SAM: When I was fifteen, when I felt like shit, like less than shit, and I couldn't stop feeling it, I'd sneak out, early in the morning, real early, like almost dark early and cold. I'd think I got to do something about this, I got to stop it, pull myself out of the shit, I'm sinking in it, I'm stinking of it, and I'd go out the window and down the road and onto the freeway and wait for someone to pull over and pick me up and then he'd drive me, sometimes way out or sometimes he'd pull into a nearby street and park under a tree, and then I'd fuck him and I'd think, I got you, I got you, I really got you, and start to feel real, feel like I could fuck the world and make it do anything I please.

BILLY *and* BOBBY *stare at* SAM *in silence.*

BILLY: There's something wrong with that.
SAM: No there's not.
BOBBY: There is.
SAM: What?
BILLY: Something I can't put my finger on.
SAM: I don't give a fuck what you think.
BOBBY: Something doesn't add up.
BILLY: Doesn't sit right.
SAM: I felt great. I felt …
BOBBY: Yeah, great.
SAM: I did. I do.
BILLY: Sure you do.
SAM: Sex is great.
BOBBY: Yeah, great.
SAM: I love sex. I love it.
BILLY: Sure you do.
SAM: When was the first time you had sex?
BILLY: You kidding me?
SAM: What?
BOBBY: You don't ask that.
BILLY: Why do you want to know that?
BOBBY: What's wrong with you?
BILLY: You don't ask that.
SAM: Okay.
BILLY: You don't.
SAM: I said okay.
BOBBY: Jesus, are you stupid or something?
SAM: It was just for something to say.
BILLY: When was the first time you had sex? Oh my God! Dumb as dog shit.
SAM: What's the big fucking deal?

BILLY: You don't fucking ask that! Got it?!

Pause. BILLY *and* BOBBY *look at* SAM.

SAM: Got it.

Silence.

BILLY: When did you?

BOBBY *thinks.*

I can't remember.

BOBBY: There's your answer, Samantha, we can't remember.

A room.

BOBBY *stands with her hands away from her body.*

BOBBY: I don't like these. I don't like them. I never wanted them. I got no use for them. They're ridiculous. Stupid. Fucking stupid things that I don't want. They're obscene. And them bits, I don't want them, they've got nothing to do with me. I used to be slim, beautiful slim, lean, all muscle, no ugly bits, no shit handles, no crappy round bits. I fucking don't want this. I never wanted this, it wasn't for me. It's a fucking mistake and I have to live with it. This mistake. This wrong. The wrongness of this. So out of luck. And this, fuck, what the hell is this? This is not mine, this is nothing to do with me, this fucking stink. This is too much. How the hell do I live with this? This bleed, this muck, this stuff that's not mine, that's got nothing to do with me, that belongs to that bitch and that bitch, not me.

A room.

BILLY: I've got great tits.
SAM: I've got great tits.
BILLY: Yeah, not bad.
SAM: Not bad! They're good.
BILLY: Who says?
SAM: I've been told lots of times. I've had them yell out of cars. I can't tell you how many times I've had men groping at them they like them that much. I've had them making gestures at them from across bars, I've …

BILLY: They're too small.
SAM: No, they're not!
BILLY: I'm letting you know they're not that good.
SAM: Fuck you, they're good.
BILLY: They're like pancakes.
SAM: They are not.
BILLY: Like squashed.
SAM: They are fucking not.
BILLY: I'm sorry to be the one telling you the truth for once.
SAM: I like them.
BILLY: That's good.
SAM: I think they're good.
BILLY: That's good.
SAM: I like them.
BILLY: Good.
SAM: Yours are perfect I suppose.
BILLY: They are.
SAM: I've got a great arse.
BILLY: I've got a great arse.
SAM: You've got no arse.
BILLY: Heart-shaped, my arse.
SAM: Heart-shaped? Forget it, you've got no bum.
BILLY: That's you. Bony arsed.
SAM: Fuck off, I'm shapely.
BILLY: Yeah, like table-leg shapely.
SAM: I've got great legs.
BILLY: I've got great legs.
SAM: You have not. I've got the hole between my thighs thing with my legs.
BILLY: You've got them cankles.
SAM: Cankles! I have not got cankles.
BILLY: You've got no sex appeal.
SAM: Bullshit! I've got sex appeal. I got so much sex appeal. I've got it like it's on tap. I've got it, I've got it alright. They can't keep their hands off me, they can't stop themselves, they love me that much, they want me and want me and want me some more. I've got so much sex appeal I …
BILLY: You've got the sex appeal of Yvonne.

SAM: Who the fuck's Yvonne?
BILLY: That fat girl in a house one time who stopped talking and looked glum, who was so so sad all the time.
SAM: I don't look like Yvonne!
BILLY: About as sexy as Yvonne.
SAM: That's you. You're Yvonne.
BILLY: No way. I'm alive. I'm on fire.
SAM: Someone should throw a bucket of water on you.
BILLY: Nothing could put me out.
SAM: I'm going to call the fire brigade.

    BOBBY *can't stand any more.*

BOBBY: Women shit me.
BILLY: Here we go.
SAM: We know, we know.
BOBBY: They don't weigh in.
BILLY: Yeah yeah.
BOBBY: Not in for the count.
SAM: Yeah yeah.

From left: Peta Brady as Sam, Nicci Wilks as Billy and Sarah Ward as Bobby in NEON Festival of Independent Theatre's 2015 production of SHIT in Melbourne. (Photo: Sebastian Bourges)

BOBBY: Don't get to play.
BILLY: Yeah yeah.
BOBBY: Don't mark the ball.
SAM: Yeah yeah.
BOBBY: Don't kick, hit, strike no goals.
SAM/BILLY: Yeah yeah.
BOBBY: With their whining and their crying and their bitching and talking shit.
SAM: Yeah well.
BOBBY: Always talking shit. My God, how much shit can they talk? They're full of it. Women are shit.
BILLY: Yeah well.
BOBBY: In their stupid little skirts or tiny fucking shorts, and their fucking high heels and their fucking fat tits. What can you say about them? Nothing.
SAM: Yeah well, that's how it is.
BOBBY: They don't do anything. They don't make anything. They don't have anything. They sit around on their arses.
SAM/BILLY: Yeah well …
BOBBY: Always wanting to be looked at, to be seen, talking too loud, talking obscene, talking like they love it up the arse, sucking cock, drinking cum, their tits being bit. Like they like it with that one and then that one, queue up, bring it on. Talking shit. They are shit.
SAM/BILLY: I'm not shit.
BOBBY: And their orange faces and, their smelly armpits and their stinking holes. God, stop cackling, stop screeching, stop their silly giggling with their tits all jiggling, thinking they're someone. They're nothing. They're shit. That's it. Shit.
SAM/BILLY: I'm not shit!
BILLY: Hey hey hey, what's with the theys?
SAM: Yeah.
BILLY: What do you mean: *They* don't do this, *they* don't do that?
SAM: Yeah.
BOBBY: They can't run. They can't fight. Can't save themselves if they tried.
SAM: I used to run.
BOBBY: Who from?
SAM: In events. I won. Lots of times.

BOBBY: But you stopped.

> As she continues, SAM and BILLY groan.

They go on about what they've not got. Not got love, not got respect, not got their kids, not got money, got nowhere to live. On and on about what's been done to them. He did this. He did that. He touched me up, he jumped me, he made me suck his cock. Who gives a shit? No-one's listening, no-one gives a fuck. It's not fair, it's not right, oh my God, get a life. Face it. You're shit, alright?

SAM/BILLY: We're not shit!
BILLY: Who's you?
BOBBY: What?
BILLY: Who are you in all them theys?
SAM: Yeah, who are you?
BILLY: You forgot?
SAM: Don't you know?
BILLY: You're them too.
SAM: How come you forgot?
BILLY: You talk like you're a bloke.
SAM: What's with that?

> Pause.

BILLY: Gone all quiet at last.
SAM: Got nothing more to say.
BILLY: Do you think you're a man?
SAM: Not really, you don't, do you?
BILLY: Oh my God, you do.

> She pokes at BOBBY's chest.

What are them then?
SAM: What do you call them?
BILLY: I call them tits.
SAM: You got a dick?
BILLY: Show us your dick.
SAM: Give us a look.
BILLY: What's wrong?
SAM: Don't be shy.
BILLY: Let me suck your dick.
SAM: Come on, big boy, get it out.

BILLY: Do you really think you're not one of us?
SAM: You can't.
BILLY: You honestly think you're not a chick?
SAM: Oh my God, / you do.
BILLY: / You do. You think you're a man, a fucking man.

Silence.

Pull down your pants.
SAM: She said, pull down your pants.
BILLY: Pull down your pants.

SAM sneaks up from behind and pulls BOBBY's trousers down to her knees.

SAM: You're no fucking different from us.
BILLY: You're a cunt. What are you?
SAM: A cunt.
BILLY: Want us to prove it to you?

She gestures with her fingers.

BOBBY mumbles inaudibly.

Didn't hear you.

Barely audible.

BOBBY: A cunt.
BILLY: I didn't hear you.
BOBBY: A cunt.
BILLY: That's right.

The sound of footsteps, high-heel ones. The footsteps falter and begin again, but this time at a faster speed. Then they resound at a run.

The three women emerge from the dark edges.

They run together, like hunting dogs.

The footsteps suddenly stop.

A room.

Something's up with SAM. She looks long and hard at BILLY.

SAM: You shouldn't of looked at him.
BILLY: I didn't.

SAM: You did.
BILLY: I didn't.
SAM: Yes you did.
BILLY: I …
BOBBY: For fuck's sake, you did. We saw you. We saw you. Alright? You did.
BILLY: It's a fucking free country. I can look at him if I want.
SAM: Why did you?
BILLY: Why not?
SAM: Because you wanted him?
BILLY: No.
SAM: Because you wanted to give Sandra the shits.
BOBBY: To make her go off her tits.
BILLY: Fuck her.
SAM: You did.
BOBBY: Well and truly.
BILLY: She gives me the shits.
SAM: What she done to you?
BILLY: She thinks she's king shit.
SAM: Bitch.
BILLY: Who you calling bitch?
SAM: We're here because of you.
BOBBY: It's true.
BILLY: No. That's not why we're here.
SAM: You started it.
BOBBY: You did.
SAM: With your looking looking.
BILLY: No.
BOBBY: You got Sandra all bothered, you got her all hot …
SAM: … under the collar.
BILLY: What's that got to do with what came later?
SAM: Because she's at Craig.
BOBBY: And at him and at him.
SAM: And then he snaps.
BOBBY: And he bashes her.
BILLY: I repeat, what's that got to do with what came later?
SAM: Craig bashing Sandra …

BOBBY: Craig smashing her ...
SAM: Stirred us up.
BOBBY: Unsettled us.
SAM: Gave us a hunger.
BILLY: A hunger?
SAM: Yeah, kind of.
BOBBY: Yeah, kind of.
BILLY: A fucking hunger?
SAM: Yeah that.
BOBBY: Exactly that.
SAM: Looking for something, anything, someone.
BOBBY: Anyone.
SAM: Anyone.
BOBBY: And she came along.
SAM: And she came along. Whoever the fuck she was.
BOBBY: Poor bitch.
SAM: Poor bitch.
BOBBY: Poor bitch.
SAM: Because of your looking.
BILLY: Shut the fuck up.
SAM: You done that to me.
BILLY: What?
SAM: You've tried to con on to all the blokes I had.
BILLY: You never had no bloke worth looking at.
SAM: I'd have a lot more if it wasn't you looking at them trying to take them all.
BILLY: Believe me, I don't look at your blokes.
SAM: Mick. You looked at him and then he didn't want me anymore.
BILLY: Mick. Looking at Mick, don't make me sick.
SAM: You can't help yourself, you slut.
BILLY: What did you call me?
SAM: A slut.
BILLY: Want to say that again.
SAM: Slut slut slut slut ...

They're in for the fight.

BILLY quickly takes the advantage. She grabs a handful of SAM's hair, pulls her head down and pushes her face into the floor.

BILLY: Want to stop?
SAM: No!

> BILLY *bangs* SAM*'s head against the floor.*

BILLY: Want to stop?
SAM: No!

> *And again.*

  No. Okay! Okay!

> BILLY *releases her.*

> SAM *nurses her head for a moment.*

  Ow! You fucking hurt me.
BILLY: Well …

> SAM *laughs.* BILLY *joins in the laughter.*

> BILLY *offers* SAM *her hand and pulls her to her feet.*

> BILLY *kisses* SAM *on the lips.*

  I love you.
SAM: I love you too.

A glimpse of SAM, BOBBY *and* BILLY *committing an horrendous act.*

A room.

SAM: Fuck fuck fuck fuck fuck fuck, oh fuck, fuck fuck fuck.
BILLY: Fuck.
BOBBY: Fuck.
SAM: Fuck fuck fuck.
BILLY: Oh fuck.
BOBBY: Oh fuck.
SAM: Fuck fuck fuck.
BILLY: That's enough.
SAM: Fuck fuck …
BILLY: Sam.
SAM: Fuck fuck …
BILLY: Sam.
SAM: Fuck fuck …
BILLY: Sam!

BOBBY: Stop.
SAM: Oh fuck. Oh fuck. Oh fuck.
BILLY: Sam, stop.
BOBBY: Settle down.
SAM: Fuck fuck fuck. What've we done?
BILLY/BOBBY: Shoosh.
SAM: What've we done?
BILLY/BOBBY: Shoosh.
SAM: Fuck fuck fuck …
BILLY/BOBBY: Shut up!

    SAM *clasps her hands over her mouth.*

BILLY: Right.
BOBBY: Right.
BILLY: Got to get our story tight.
BOBBY: Real tight.
BILLY: No, we're right, we're right.
BOBBY: We're not right, we're fucked, mate, we're night-night.
BILLY: Let me think.
BOBBY: Yeah yeah you think, have a fucking think.
SAM: It's wrong, it's wrong, it's wrong. What we gone done?
BILLY: Shut the fuck up!
SAM: Oh my God, what she done? She done nothing, nothing.
BILLY: She was there.
SAM: Yeah.
BILLY: Just there.
BOBBY: Yeah.
SAM: In the wrong place …
BOBBY: At the wrong time.
SAM: Yeah.

    BILLY *thinks.*

BILLY: Who seen us? No-one. Who knows? No-one.
BOBBY: Us. We know.
BILLY: So? You're not going to go blabbing. You're not going to say nothing? I'm zipped. Nothing to worry about. That's it. Something just …
ALL: Snapped.

BILLY: Done now.
BOBBY/SAM: Done.
BILLY: Can't go back.
BOBBY/SAM: Can't go back.
SAM: We're shit.
BILLY: We're right.
SAM: We're shit.
BILLY: We're right.
SAM: We're shit.
BILLY: We're right.
BOBBY: We're fucked.

In a police line-up, the three women turn: profile, face-on, profile.

A room.

BILLY: They'll split us.
BOBBY: For sure.
SAM: No they won't, will they?
BILLY: For sure.
BOBBY: They'll divide us.
SAM: No way!
BILLY: You never would of done it if it wasn't for her or her they'll say.
BOBBY: Who was it gave the word?
BILLY: Who's the bad apple in the barrel?
BOBBY: Who's the leader in this?
BILLY: Whose was the first kick?
BOBBY: They'll ask us to spill our guts.
SAM: I'd never do that.
BOBBY: Be a rat?
SAM: I'd never.
BILLY: Lots of rats say that.
SAM: I'd never. We're in this together.
BOBBY: They'll split us. They'll send us far far away.
BILLY: No phone calls, no contact, no nothing.
SAM: They can't do that.
BOBBY: They can do whatever they want with us.
SAM: I'm not going anywhere without you.

BILLY: You're going wherever they want you to.
SAM: No. No fucking way. I want to be with you.
BOBBY: They decide. Not you.
SAM: No. I don't want to be without you.
BILLY: We're no good for you, they'll say.
SAM: Yes you are. You're good for me.
BOBBY: A bad influence, they'll say.
SAM: No. They're wrong.
BOBBY: They don't care.
SAM: I do. Do something. Tell them. It can't be.
BILLY: Sam, what did you think? They'd keep us together?
SAM: Yes. I did.
BOBBY: They'll split us.
BILLY: We won't see each other again.

Silence.

BOBBY: Are you crying?

Pause.

Are you?
BILLY: No.
BOBBY: You look like you're crying.
SAM: You do.
BILLY: No.
BOBBY: You are.
SAM: You are.
BILLY: No.
BOBBY: You're crying.

The three women click their fingers once. They turn and walk together a few steps, then click again. They peel off and exit in different directions.

END

www.currency.com.au

Visit Currency Press' website now to:

- Buy your books online
- Browse through our full list of titles, from plays to screenplays, books on theatre, film and music, and more
- Choose a play for your school or amateur performance group by cast size and gender
- Obtain information about performance rights
- Find out about theatre productions and other performing arts news across Australia
- For students, read our study guides
- For teachers, access syllabus and other relevant information
- Sign up for our email newsletter

The performing arts publisher

www.ingramcontent.com/pod-product-compliance
Lightning Source LLC
Chambersburg PA
CBHW040307170426
43194CB00022B/2925